THE FARMER AS

The Farmer as Manager

TONY GILES

*Senior Lecturer in Agricultural Economics
and Director of the Farm Management Unit,
University of Reading*

MALCOLM STANSFIELD

*Lecturer in Farm Management
and Deputy Director of the Farm Management Unit,
University of Reading*

London
GEORGE ALLEN & UNWIN
Boston   Sydney

First published in 1980

This book is copyright under the Berne Convention. All rights are reserved. Apart from any fair dealing for the purpose of private study, research, criticism or review, as permitted under the Copyright Act, 1956, no part of this publication may be reproduced, stored in a retrieval system, or transmitted, in any form or by any means, electronic, electrical, chemical, mechanical, optical, photocopying, recording or otherwise, without the prior permission of the copyright owner. Enquiries should be sent to the publishers at the undermentioned address:

GEORGE ALLEN & UNWIN LTD
40 Museum Street, London WC1A 1LU

© A. K. Giles and J. M. Stansfield, 1980

British Library Cataloguing in Publication Data

Giles, Tony
　The farmer as manager.
　1. Farm management — Great Britain
　I. Title II. Stansfield, Malcolm
　658'.93'0941　　　S562.G7　　　79-40956

ISBN 0-04-658228-2
ISBN 0-04-658229-0 Pbk

Typeset in 11 on 12 point Baskerville
and printed in Great Britain
by Unwin Brothers Limited, Old Woking, Surrey

To all those who at one time or another have helped us to develop our views and who have encouraged us to write them down.

Acknowledgements

The authors are especially grateful to Harold Casey, Richard Clarke, Graham Dalton, Michael Dart, Edgar Thomas, Don Salmon and Stuart Wragg, all of whom, in their different capacities, have given helpful comments on either the layout or the contents of this book – without trying to persuade us to write something substantially different from our original intentions.

We would also like to thank Mrs Audrey Collins, Miss Sue Pipe and Miss Carol Rees who, between them, have typed and retyped the manuscript; our families who, while it was being written, forfeited a summer holiday, with hardly a murmur; and, finally, John Churchill and Roger Jones, of George Allen & Unwin, who guided us patiently through the inevitable hiccups.

TONY GILES
MALCOLM STANSFIELD

Contents

PART I *Introduction*

1. About this book — page 3
2. About management — 9

PART II *Management functions*

3. Setting objectives — 19
4. Planning — 30
5. Decision making — 43
6. Control — 59

PART III *What has to be managed*

7. Production — 73
8. Buying and selling — 97
9. Finance — 113
10. Staff — 143

PART IV *The manager*

11. Managing the manager — 159
12. Acquiring information — 170
13. Priorities — 181
14. Summary and conclusions — 186

Index — 197

Part I
INTRODUCTION

The authors have deliberately chosen *profit* as the note on which to introduce this book

1
About this book

INTRODUCTION

It is unlikely that many farmers, or indeed many other kinds of businessmen, would suggest that profit is the sole reason for their being in business. In many cases it may not even be the most important reason; but equally, many farmers would include profit high in their list of reasons for farming.

In farming, as elsewhere, profits are significant in a number of ways. First, they *measure* the overall success with which a business is being managed. They permit judgements to be made about the degree of that success, or the lack of it, and in this way they help to direct thinking and to influence morale. Secondly, profits *provide a reward* to those who invest capital into and manage a business and thereby provide the incentive to continue. And thirdly, profits provide part, at least, of the funds from which *future expansion and development is made possible*. In a word, profits encourage and permit *survival* and, in the belief that survival is ultimately what successful management is about, we have deliberately chosen profit as the note on which to introduce this book.

Those who are familiar with farm profits will know that they can be highly variable between both different farming years and different farms. Indeed, there is no reason at all why different kinds and sizes of farms should expect to enjoy a similar profit potential. Even within a reasonably homogeneous group of farm businesses (and, of course, no two are alike) there is usually a wide gap between the best and the worst financial results obtained in any one year. This phenomenon is not peculiar to farming although the amount of data published about the industry may well mean that we know more about the situation in agriculture than we do in other sectors of the economy. All of that data, however, whether it concerns whole-farm businesses or individual farm enterprises, points to a wide dispersion around the average, and draws attention to the 'performance gap', as we call it.

Any attempt to discover the underlying reasons for this situation immediately revolves around two broad sets of issues: physical resources and human attributes. Clearly, the amount of land involved, its inherent quality and flexibility, and the natural advantages it enjoys from climatic conditions, will all have a big influence on the profit potential of any particular farm business. In the long term each of these three aspects of the land farmed can be altered or modified: additional land can be acquired; good husbandry methods can improve soil structure and fertility; and irrigation may add to normal rainfall. In the short term, however, (and the short term can become surprisingly long!) all of these things are relatively fixed, and it is left to the human element – management – to do the best that it can with the resources it has. Again it could be argued that in the short term the quality of the management input is often relatively fixed. Because of widely differing family backgrounds, self employed farmers embark on their individual farming careers from a wide range of starting points. In no respect is this more true than in regard to financial circumstances, and balance sheets, like soil fertility, have a habit of changing only slowly. Farmers and farm managers also enter the industry with a basic education followed, increasingly, by some form of specialised agricultural training. From then on, learning by experience plays a dominant part in any manager's life, and his capacity for personal and professional growth, with all that stems from it, may well be the most flexible element in the whole complex which makes up any farm business. Indeed, we would go further, and suggest that it is in *this* element – the capacity for personal and professional growth on the part of the manager – where the greatest opportunity for continual development and improvement of resources is likely to be found.

FOR WHOM IS THIS BOOK INTENDED?

This book has been written primarily for those farmers and farm managers who are not only capable of such development but who also want to achieve it. It must also be stressed that it has been written for those who actually manage farms, or who one day intend to, and not for those who teach, research into, or advise on farm management – although, naturally, we would hope that some of them may also find it of interest.

It should also be emphasised that the book is about farming only in the sense that it is about the *management* of farms, and frequently it will be argued by us – while acknowledging that every industry has its own special technical problems, and farming may feel it has more than its share of them – that management is management *wherever* it is practised. However, this book is not about farm management in any narrow husbandry sense. The reader will be disappointed if he looks for guidance on the management of individual farm enterprises. There will be even more disappointment if he looks for a broad treatise on agricultural economics or a detailed account of esoteric operational research techniques. In this context it does seem to us that many earlier books that have appeared under the 'farm management' label have not really been about farm management in the way that we see it, i.e. as something undertaken by those who manage farms. We are not criticising those books, but merely stating our own position; and here, although husbandry, economics and business techniques are not totally ignored, the emphasis is on those issues and problems, other than manual ones, with which managers of farms are constantly confronted. In particular we have tried to concern ourselves with those aspects of management which seem to us to worry farm managers most and which they find most difficult to order in their minds.

WHAT HAS BEEN EXCLUDED FROM THIS BOOK?

Before saying something about the layout and content of the book, we would like to point out some of the omissions. They stem partly from our knowledge of the community for whom we have written, partly from the kind of book we have wanted to offer them (i.e. one to be *read*), and partly from our own ignorance – coupled with a firm belief that specialised topics are better dealt with by specialists in specialised books. Also, although writing in the United Kingdom in the late 1970's, we have aimed to write a book that will interest an international farming readership and that will not quickly become outdated.

With these objectives in mind, and having already established that the book is neither about husbandry nor economics, we make no apology for having omitted, or only touched lightly upon, topics which are peculiar to this country at this point of time. Legal, policy and certain fiscal matters, such as taxation, fall squarely into this category.

We also decided at the outset that, so far as possible, we would avoid too many examples of business management techniques. This is not to suggest for a moment that they have no place in farming; we know of course that they have, and that when they are required, farmers can either use them themselves or rely on advisers and consultants, depending on the circumstances. Nevertheless we have excluded them for three reasons: first, because, in our opinion, they do not fall into the category of 'those issues and problems with which managers of farms are constantly confronted', and which this book is primarily about; secondly, because, even if that were not the case, we would merely be repeating material that has been made available in other books (in the UK, for example, by Barnard & Nix and by Norman & Coote [See Further Reading, Chs 4 & 5]); and thirdly, because we wanted to write a book that will be read: *read* rather than *used* as a manual.

But that is more than enough about what is not in the book; let us turn for a moment to what is.

THE LAYOUT AND CONTENT OF THE BOOK

The reader will find that no standard pattern is adopted in each chapter. We have collaborated closely when planning each chapter and it has then been written in whatever way seemed appropriate, sometimes by one of us, sometimes by the other and sometimes jointly. Depending upon the subject matter, therefore, some chapters will be more concerned with principles of management or with ways of thinking about such nebulous concepts as 'setting objectives' or 'decision making', and others will be more concerned with practical matters such as production and man-management. Sometimes there is a combination of theory illustrated by practice. In the main, however, the reader will find that he is offered ways of thinking about management and managerial problems rather than answers to specific farm problems. We have tried to offer *directions*, but *decisions* are left to the reader.

Turning now to the order of the book, the chapters have been arranged so that after this introductory one, there is one which considers the overall role of farm managers. There are then four which deal, in turn, with certain basic management functions: setting objectives, planning, decision making and control. These chapters are followed by four which discuss the principal areas over which management has to operate in any business: production, marketing, financing and staffing. And before the concluding chapter, there are three which concentrate on the manager himself: on how he organises himself, how he acquires information and how he sets priorities.

At the beginning of each chapter diagrammatic presentation has been used in an attempt to assist the reader in the retention of the main line of thought being presented. For the same reason each chapter ends with a series of simple questions. They are not intended to be an examination for the reader but rather to check on the extent to which the principal message contained in each chapter has been understood and remembered. Occasional reference back to these diagrams and questions might be a convenient way of recalling material that has been read. It may even provide the basis for discussion at farmers' meetings. A final chapter provides a summary and our concluding thoughts.

Apart from the first and the last ones, each chapter is accompanied by a number of annotated references to other work, especially where the further elaboration of an idea or technique would have been beyond the intended scope and length of this book. But these references have been very strictly limited in number; we know that we are addressing busy people.

WRITING THE BOOK

Finally, in this first chapter we would like, on a more personal note, to add a word or two about how the book came to be written in the first place. This may throw some light on why it follows the style that it does.

Many books written by academics have their origins in lecture notes. For us the origins have been slightly different, coming instead from the countless conversations that we have had with farmers throughout this country and in others. Sometimes these conversations have been face to face with individuals, but very often they have been with audiences at farmers' meetings. Between us we have been involved in several hundred such meetings: with professional associations and with farming unions, at conferences and discussion groups, in colleges and church halls, in hotels, pubs and in farm houses.

Throughout these experiences, we have been working in close proximity to each other at Reading University – one as an agricultural economist specialising in farm business management and the other actually 'doing the job' on the University's farms – and have become aware that, despite our different standpoints, we have often been thinking and saying the same kind of things. It was this common ground, stemming largely from evening speaking and from our work in the University, which led to our decision to write this particular kind of book. We see it, therefore, not as a text book covering the entire field of farm management, but rather as a collection of thoughts, based on some of the topics that we have discussed with farming audiences and students up and down the country. If the reader receives any help at all from what he reads here, we will feel that we have been able to repay some of the benefits, friendship and hospitality that we have both been privileged to enjoy on these occasions.

2
About management

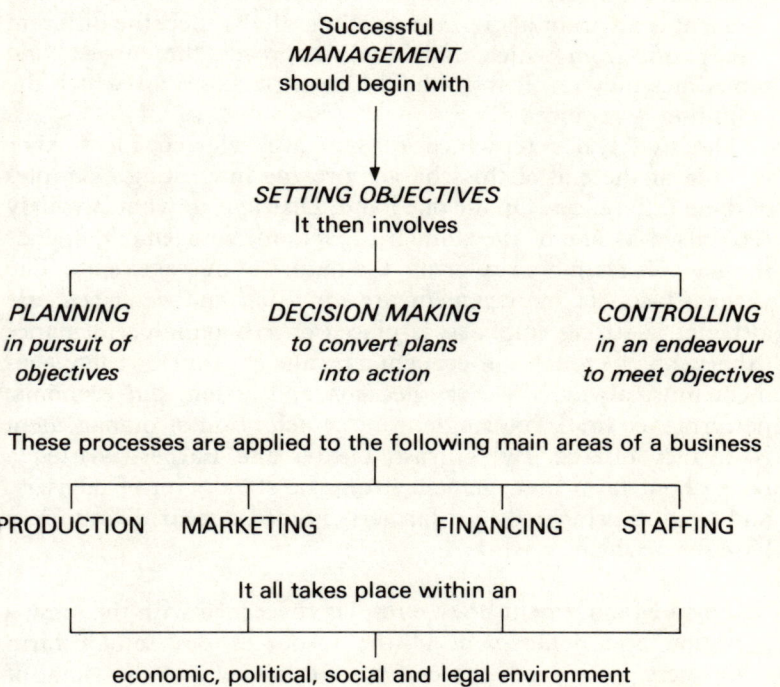

A DEFINITION OF MANAGEMENT

Agreeing on definitions of any subject can be a hair splitting and time consuming business. It usually requires compromises by everybody involved and often produces results that please nobody; defining management is no exception.

There are probably as many different definitions of management as there are authors who have written about it and managers who practise it. These differences arise for a variety of reasons. Sometimes they arise from profitless debate about whether management is an art or a science; sometimes they reflect the different standpoints from which individuals approach the subject; and sometimes they result from the different purposes for which the definition is required.

The two books to which readers are referred for further reading at the end of this chapter provide interesting examples of these differences. On the one hand, Drucker, in what is widely recognised as one of the standard texts on management, spends three whole chapters exploring 'the nature of management'. The various facets of management are *discussed* and *described* and although a strong emphasis is placed on economic performance ('there may be great non-economic results . . . (but) . . . management must always, in every decision and action, put economic performance first'), no single, concise definition of management is, in fact, offered. By contrast, Dexter and Barber, writing a book about farm management, from the standpoint of advisers, and writing principally for farmers, needed a clear definition; a base from which to work.

> 'Farm Management [they wrote] is concerned with the organisation and deployment of the resources put into a farm business – the land, the capital, the labour and that item of over-riding importance, the ability and skills of the individual farmer. It is not, in our opinion, [they continue] concerned with the purely technical matters in farming, nor, on the other hand, is it concerned with the best way of giving the orders to the staff at seven o'clock in the morning. These questions do arise but they are subordinate to the main consideration of organising a farm for higher profit.'

These two books were written from very different standpoints and with different purposes and audiences in mind. Nevertheless they do demonstrate agreement on one fundamental task of management; that of, 'putting economic performance first' and of 'organising a farm for higher profits'.

We have already made our own position about the importance of profits quite clear at the very outset of this book. Profits permit and encourage survival. They are not the only thing that matters, but, without them, insolvency may follow and then it is too late for anything else to matter. It is also our belief that farms are likely to be successfully managed, and profits generated, if certain general principles of management are understood and applied to farm businesses, just as they should be to other businesses and organisations. This is not to say that we wish to belittle the importance of good husbandry and of doing things well technically. On the contrary, it is very important to 'do things well', and it will seldom, in fact, be in conflict with doing things profitably. It is common knowledge that it is the last few eggs, piglets, litres of milk or kilos of corn which produce the profit.

We will return to this subject in Chapter 7, which deals with production, but at this stage we wish to emphasise our belief that *too much* preoccupation with the *purely* technical and with day-to-day matters could be dangerous if it is at the expense of the more strategic, commercial and human aspects of management. It may even be debatable whether it is helpful, in this respect, to think about 'farm management' as a subject in its own right at all. It may be more rewarding to think simply in terms of *management applied to farms*, with the technical problems of farming falling into their appropriate place alongside all the others.

With these thoughts in mind, our own working definition of management is, therefore, deliberately stripped of any agricultural connotations, and is as follows:

Management is a comprehensive activity, involving the combination and co-ordination of human, physical and financial resources, in a way which produces a commodity or a service which is both wanted and can be offered at a price which will be paid, while making the working environment for those involved agreeable and acceptable.

This definition may be a little lengthy, but it is deliberately so, in order to serve our particular purpose. It draws attention to a number of issues which we believe to be important and which a shorter definition could not encompass. First, it shows that management cannot be conceived as having narrow boundaries. Depending upon the size of an organisation, the delegation of various aspects of management may or may not be possible. In most small businesses – which the majority of farms are – the opportunities for the delegation of management are strictly limited. But delegation or not, *top management* ultimately has the responsibility for all that goes on. Management can never, therefore, be less than a comprehensive process.

Secondly, management is concerned with *combination*: with the combination of a number of different and separate factors of production – land, labour and capital – into an effective and viable production unit. The classical economic questions about production – what to produce, in what combination and by what methods – are at the heart of this aspect of the manager's task.

Thirdly, our definition points to the need for managers to be market orientated. Attention needs to be kept carefully focused on an *end product*, in the knowledge that the product (or service) must be wanted by consumers and that it must be supplied at a price they are willing to pay. The mind is thus immediately focused not just on production, but on effective production in economic terms and that means the long term survival of the business on a sound financial basis.

And, finally, there is emphasis on the human factor. We believe that in any business situation the provision of agreeable and acceptable working conditions may be as important an element in the long term survival of that business as is profit itself. The importance of this most influential and variable of all resources cannot be overstressed and we make no apology, therefore, for the final clause of our definition.

CLOTHING THE DEFINITION

If a definition is a necessary starting point in the discussion of any subject, it is just as necessary to move quickly beyond it and to develop and clothe the initial statement. It is all very well to use academic-sounding phrases like 'the co-ordination of human, physical and financial resources', but *what does it mean* – or

Clothing the definition

more important still, what *should* it mean – in terms of actually managing an organisation? What picture of management as a practical task emerges from the clothing of our definition?

Attempts to describe the work of managers usually tend to fall into one of two categories: the *prescriptive* and the *descriptive*. The first of these two approaches concentrates mainly on what managers *ought* to do, and the second on what they *do* do. This book probably falls somewhere between the two approaches with, in most chapters, some combination of *principles* and *practice*. This particular chapter, however, is more concerned with principles and when we move beyond our definition the framework of management which emerges in our minds is the one shown at the front of this chapter and on which the sequence of the book is based. No diagram of this kind can be regarded as sacrosanct. It is simply a personal view of how the manager's task can be helpfully envisaged. Such a diagram will be a disservice if it is thought to reflect the whole story, or if it suggests that either the main *processes* depicted (setting objectives, planning, decision making and controlling) or the main *sectors* of the business (production, marketing, financing and staffing) are as separate and independent of each other as the diagram suggests. All of those involved in farm management will know that this is not the case. However, such a diagram does have the merit of identifying the key areas of responsibility and activity to which the manager of any business has to address himself. In addition it serves the purpose of keeping each of these responsibilities and activities in perspective, and of not losing sight of the comprehensiveness of the manager's task. At the risk of repetition, therefore, the key words of the diagram are shown again here:

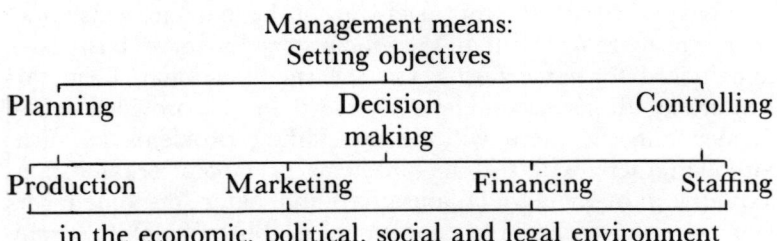

This picture is intended to suggest to the reader that effective management *should* begin with a careful consideration of *objec*-

tives, and that without this no clear directions can be followed and no really meaningful assessment can be made of subsequent achievement. That particular subject is considered in detail in Chapter 3. Assuming, for the moment, however, that it is possible to identify and, preferably, to quantify certain objectives, then certain clear courses of action are necessary if those objectives are to be achieved. First, *plans* must be devised in each relevant area of the organisation or business concerned which permit the stated objectives to be pursued. Those plans must then be put into operation, or kept in operation, as a result of *decisions* that managers must take. Indeed, some writers on management have been inclined to equate the central task of management with the decision making process – a view that we shall consider in the appropriate chapter. However, things do not stop there. Setting objectives, devising plans and making decisions will all have been wasted effort if care is not taken to ensure that what is required to happen does in fact happen. If it does not, then the reasons for this need to be known and understood and wherever possible corrective action needs to be taken. In other words, *control* must be exercised.

To a large extent it is having the responsibility for these matters – setting objectives, planning, decision making and controlling – which characterises the manager's role. He will be required to exercise these responsibilities in respect to each main section or area of his business and for many businesses this means: production, marketing, financing and staffing. If, in all of this. the manager whom we have in mind is not the owner of the business, he undertakes the stewardship of the business on behalf of its owners. But if he is the owner, then he will, instead, accept the final risk for the capital that is at stake.

It is appreciated that this brief view of the manager's task may represent more or less than the whole story for many businesses and indeed for some farms. On the small one-man farm, for instance, with perhaps no labour other than that provided by the farmer himself, there will be no staffing problems as such, although there will still be problems of labour organisation. Equally, in many large organisations and, again, on some farms (for example, those run by educational establishments) there may be a research and development section quite separate from any of the four business sections considered here. For many situations, however, it is believed that this fourfold division is appropriate.

It is also appreciated that there is a close interaction between each of these sections. They are not as independent as the diagram may suggest. Decisions about what to produce and when and how to produce it have immediate and obvious repercussions on marketing arrangements, on capital requirements and on the number and quality of staff to be employed. In a similar way, decisions which relate primarily to questions of capital supply or to the availability of labour will have an important influence on production possibilities. The examples of such interactions could be continued endlessly.

But finally, in this outline of management it must be said that no business and, therefore by definition, no farm, exists or operates in a vacuum. Social, legal, political and economic constraints sometimes emanating from forces (especially economic forces) well beyond national boundaries, are constantly affecting the freedom of managers to manage in an unfettered way. Increasingly it becomes the task of managers to try to understand and to adapt to these changing forces. Any kind of detailed analysis of these forces is well beyond the scope of this book, but such matters as the way in which prices and costs are influenced by international markets, the prevailing climate for borrowing funds, the effect of legal constraints in the field of employment, social responsibilities in respect to such questions as pollution, and the influence of purely political considerations on national farming policies and international agreements, are just some of the more obvious examples of the various influences which combine to create the environment in which managers have to manage. Any belief by farmers that they are unique in this respect would be mistaken. Such influences affect the whole business community. Not many managers will need reminding that these influences are real, that they are usually unavoidable and that, more often than not, they just have to be lived with. At the end of the day, farm managers, like all other managers, must simply get on and manage.

SOME QUESTIONS RELATING TO THIS CHAPTER

(1) Can you reproduce, without looking at it, the diagrammatic view of management presented at the beginning of this chapter? (If not, have another look at it and try to reproduce it tomorrow.)

(2) How would you define management?
(3) Do you agree that, 'successful management should begin with setting objectives'?
(4) Do you think the words 'production', 'marketing', 'financing' and 'staffing' adequately describe the main areas of activity that exist in most farm businesses? If not, what alternative description would you suggest?
(5) Do you think a farmer – manager has more to gain from joining a discussion group comprised of other farm managers or of managers of other kinds of business?
(6) What aspects of management do you personally find most difficult?

A GUIDE TO SELECTED FURTHER READING

Drucker, P. F. 1968. *The Practice of Management*. London: Heinemann; London: Pan Books.
  One of the standard management texts. Don't try to read it all at once; start with the Introduction for a valuable insight into 'the nature of management'. His more recent book, *Management*, also published by Pan Books, in 1979, would be equally valuable.

Dexter, K. and D. Barber 1961. *Farming for Profits*. West Drayton, Middlesex: Penguin Books; London: Associated Iliffe Press (1967).
  Despite being nearly twenty years old, the early chapters do not date. Read Chapter 1 (What's it all about?) and you will want to read on.

Part II
MANAGEMENT FUNCTIONS

3
Setting objectives

The jigsaw of personal and professional objectives

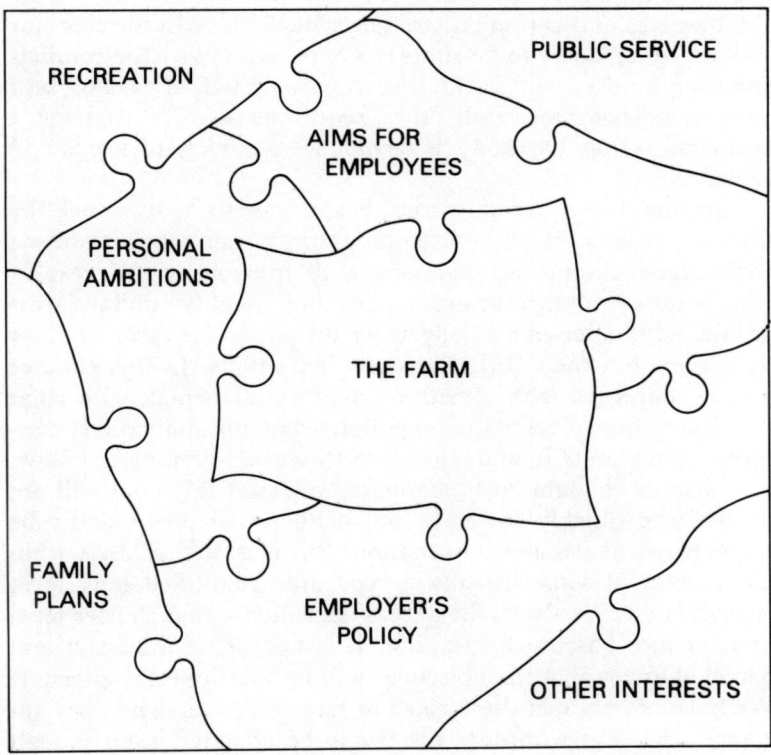

THE NEED FOR OBJECTIVES

With it now clear why and how this book has been written, and what it is about, we can safely turn our attention to the first and, no doubt, one of the most important parts of any manager's job: the setting of objectives.

It is increasingly accepted that it is important for any organisation to take a periodic look at its broad objectives for a limited number of years ahead, say three, four or five years. This helps to give the organisation itself a purpose; it provides the individuals in the organisation with a common goal and it minimises the risks of going off at too many tangents.

Objectives in this context, are never likely to be in the singular and are never likely to be simple. There will always be conflicts and compromises, and profit, important as it will always be, will have to be balanced with other requirements. 'To manage a business,' writes Drucker, 'is to balance a variety of needs and goals.'

Farming, like other industries, has its yardsticks by which the financial results for any particular trading year can be assessed and judged. Simple comparisons with previous years' results, with results drawn from groups of other roughly similar farms or even with tailor-made budgets for the particular farm, all have their uses; but they also have their limitations. In this chapter we are concerned with something more fundamental: with what a business has to offer; its potential; what the individuals concerned want out of it, and what path forward it is going to follow.

Clarity of thought on fundamental issues of this kind will not be achieved quickly or easily and neither will they usually be achieved without some consultation. But it is only really within the context of some broadly agreed and quantified long term objectives – or 'goals' as they are often called – that shorter term performance has much meaning. It is our belief that part and parcel of any manager's objectives will be a desire to be effective. We have not yet met the farmer or farm manager who does not want to be, and who does not try to be effective, even though some of them may not be. But we also believe that it is difficult to talk about effectiveness or the lack of it – about success or failure – without some reference back to the kind of long term objectives that this chapter is about.

As well as being a very important aspect of management,

setting objectives is also a notoriously difficult one as those who have tried to grapple with it will know. It is difficult because it is elusive and complicated; it is always moving away from you, always involving conflicting strands of thought and frequently defying attempts to be precise. It also requires concentration, and most of us know only too well how difficult that is, especially if (like many farmers) we have become accustomed to constant interruptions and to a fragmentation of the working day. None of us needs reminding of how easy it is to put off jobs that we find difficult, particularly if they are not pressing. What we cannot stress too strongly, however, is that although there may be jobs that are queueing up to be attended to, there are unlikely to be jobs that are more important to the long term survival of a business than thinking seriously about where it is going and how it is going to get there. That, in essence, is what setting objectives is about. It must from time to time be done, despite the many deterrents that may stand in the way; and it would, in our opinion, be unfortunate if farmers and farm managers ever felt that they were faced with more difficulties and deterrents in this respect than their counterparts in other sectors of the economy.

DETERMINING OBJECTIVES

We can imagine the reader at this stage having no difficulty in agreeing with the need to have objectives. It is so abundantly sensible to think in this way. But equally we can imagine him pondering hard over how to actually set about the exercise. The difficulties and the deterrents have been referred to. They are real. Most of us really do feel too busy to deal with anything that is not urgent, that we do not quite know how to start, and which, into the bargain, threatens to put us personally on the rack.

In recent years **management by objectives** (hereafter referred to as MBO) has gained ground throughout many industries and organisations as perhaps the most comprehensive and helpful approach to this apparently daunting task. We have already said, in the first chapter, that this book will not concern itself with techniques, but in this case we make no apology for saying a little about the subject. After all, it is specifically and justifiably claimed for MBO that it is *not* a technique; that it is a way of thinking about the *whole* management process and about a *whole* business or organisation. That makes it totally relevant to the thinking that underlies this chapter.

For the reader who is encouraged to seek detailed help from this approach we recommend, in particular, the British Institute of Management's Newsheet, and Humble's small book on 'Improving Business Results', both listed at the end of this chapter. It will be sufficient for us to say here that the essence of MBO includes:

(a) discussions, over a period of time, by an appropriately chosen small group of people concerned with the management of a business, including, often, somebody from outside the business itself, e.g. an adviser;
(b) full discussions of the external environment in which the business is operating and the opportunities that are available to it;
(c) careful analysis of the resources available to the business and the possibilities and constraints that, therefore, exist within it;
(d) clear statements, acceptable to all concerned, about where, in the longer term, the business is aiming to be, and how, in the shorter term, it plans to get there;
(e) an acceptance by all concerned of the performance levels that are assumed in the plans, and a commitment to achieve them;
(f) the quantification of as much of the plans as possible;
(g) a recognition of the 'key results' areas of the business, in which it is very important to get good results, either, narrowly, in terms of performance within a particular unit or section of a business, or more broadly, (as Drucker suggests in The Practice of Management) in areas of strategic importance, e.g. marketing, employee – employer relations;
(h) an adequate control system in order to monitor, correct and adjust plans and objectives;
(i) a willingness, periodically, to reconsider, re-plan, re-state and re-dedicate.

There is much more to be read and said about management by objectives than this, but we believe that in the context of farming and managers of farms, this list of nine points embraces its essential philosophy. Many successful farmers would no doubt claim that they have always done these things and had thought in this way, but less formally and without calling it MBO. We have no doubt, from our experience, that they are right. But equally, from our experience, we have no doubt that the formality of MBO as outlined here, and applied periodically to the whole business, does have something *extra* to offer even to the most progressive farmers and farm managers, and that there are many others for whom this approach would offer an almost totally new and beneficial dimension to their management skills.

We would not wish to be accused of over-enthusing in this matter. Indeed it is important, in the management world, that new techniques or approaches to problems are seen for what they are and are neither hailed as panaceas nor rejected out of hand as the latest gimmick. MBO is, of course, no longer new, and it would be an exaggeration to pretend that it has had anything resembling widespread application in the farming industry. We believe, however, that this is a pity and that it should not be gradually lost sight of as another gimmick that came and went. We would like to see more serious examples of its application than we know of, albeit in a style that is both relevant and acceptable to the industry.

The right approach, for instance, might call for a farmhouse meeting on rather a formal basis with objective setting as the sole item on the agenda. The form of the meeting and numbers attending will vary considerably according to the size and complexity of the business. With the small family unit, discussions may involve only the farmer and his wife whereas with the large company, the directors would ideally be joined by senior managers as well as consultants. In the family business where two or three generations are actively involved, the chairman might well have an important role to fulfil. More than one session will be required in order to agree a series of goals but the outcome should be a list of what is to be achieved and when it is to be achieved.

Approached in this way we can see several important benefits that the underlying philosophy of MBO, however informally applied, can offer the farming industry. There are four benefits, in particular, that we would like to mention briefly.

THE ADVANTAGES OF THE MBO APPROACH

First, under this heading, there is the importance of confronting oneself with what we choose to call 'square one' questions. To those who are not steeped in the jargon and style of modern business management techniques – and that may include a large proportion of our readers – the answers to questions like: 'What business are you in?' or, 'Who are our customers?' might seem so obvious, or so irrelevant to getting on with the job in hand, as to be a waste of time. And yet these are precisely the kind of questions which may help to clarify thinking across a broad spectrum of possibilities; to eliminate the unimportant and impractical; and to concentrate thinking on those areas of activity on which success is most likely to depend, i.e. on the key results areas. If the value of trying to answer basic questions of this kind is in doubt it is worth noting that Robert Townsend (in Up The Organisation) describes how his company took six months to agree on a simple twenty-three word objective that he says, 'was simple enough that we didn't have to write it down ... (but) ... it included a definition of our business ... (and) ... let us put the blinders on ourselves'. Don't be frightened, therefore, especially in these days when clear notions of just where farming begins and ends are becoming less and less easy to identify, to spend time reflecting on such basic questions as: what business you are in, who your customers are, what scale and kind of operation you envisage managing, and, broadly speaking, what kind of returns you seek. Everything else will build on the answers to these questions. It will be a salutary exercise and you will not manage it on your own.

Secondly, there is the advantage of a periodic and thorough consideration of the resources at your disposal. Again this may seem to be so obvious as not to require any special attention. But a thorough appraisal and understanding of the variability and the flexibility of the resources at your command will be at the heart of all forward planning. Constraints on the opportunities that you can grasp will be provided more by those resources than by anything else. Land, labour and capital are all available to you in limited amounts and each will usually be far from homogeneous in character. The variability and potential, for instance, of different soil types within the farm boundary and the extent to which that potential can be influenced by the application of technology; the skill and experience of your staff; the quality and flexibility of fixed capital equipment, and the availability of liquid (or near liquid) capital: all of these things will have an important influence on what is possible and what is not. Their potential and their alternative uses should not be taken for granted.

Thirdly, when carrying out this kind of appraisal it would be wrong for any manager to fall into the trap of believing that he, himself, was not part of the parcel of resources that he manages; and a very important part into the bargain. We will discuss this topic more fully in Chapter 11. It is sufficient at this stage simply to recognise this fact, and the importance of management as an influence, for good or bad, on the effectiveness of other staff and the general conduct of any business. A serious exercise in self appraisal is, therefore, a very special part of the wider examination of the resources just discussed. An honest appreciation of one's own personal aims and ambitions, as well as one's talents and limitations will be important ingredients in setting realistic and obtainable objectives. It will not be easy and, again, it will almost certainly be unachievable without the stimulation of discussion with others.

Fourth on our list is a consideration of the so-called external environment. This is in contrast to the internal environment discussed in the previous paragraph. Equally important, but perhaps more difficult to be at all precise about, it consists of those factors, national and international, that are largely economic and political in character, and that provide the environment within which any business must operate. No business operates in isolation. Understanding that environment, in all its complexity, is beyond most of us. But being aware of the more obvious commercial and political forces and trends at work, and being alert to the opportunities and constraints that they may present to your particular business, is essential. It is not an easy job. It calls for an awareness which, fortunately, we believe many farmers seem to have built-in as an almost instinctive part of their make up. Selective reading, listening and discussion all play their part in this process, the accumulated results of which should certainly find their place in any overall review of a firm's objectives. The application of MBO will help to focus attention on this aspect of management.

THE DIFFICULTIES OF THE MBO APPROACH

In advocating the approach of management by objectives and drawing attention to some of the advantages that it can offer, we are not unmindful of the difficulties that are involved and of its limitations. The difficulties were alluded to earlier in the chapter. It is an elusive and complicated exercise, always involving conflicting strands of thought. These conflicts can take several forms.

First, there is the conflict between time periods, between the short and the long terms. These periods are not easily defined and perhaps there is no need to define them too precisely. It is sufficient to remember that the short term is usually confined to a year or two, at the most, while the long term embraces a number of years beyond which it may not be very meaningful to think, somewhere between five and at the very most ten years. What is certain is that there will sometimes be conflict between a *desire to make gradual progress* towards long term objectives and the *need to contend with more immediate* short term objectives and problems. The two will often compete for time and for capital and there may be no escape from this situation. It may be an irritation, but it is a situation that must be accepted. Drucker warns us that the nature of a particular business, and of different sectors within a particular business, will have an influence on how far ahead objectives can reasonably be set and on what constitutes the short or the long term. In a farming context, the gradual building up of a dairy herd and the installation of accompanying buildings and equipment may be a clear long term objective. The need, however, to improve the performance within the existing herd, at its existing size, or to get more cows quickly in order to improve cash flows and profits, may be more pressing short term objectives, the achievement of which might easily defer the achievement of the longer term objective. What is important in this kind of situation is the ability of management to identify priorities, a subject we give special space to in a later chapter. Judgement will be required and so will flexibility. It will always be important to be looking ahead, to the technology of five years time, but not to the jeopardy of what needs to be done well today. Too much concentration on long term possibilities at the expense of short term necessities is a not uncommon reason for disappointing results. A balance, as in most things, is what is required.

A balance is also required in the conflict between a manager's professional and personal lives. The complexity of this kind of conflict is one that few of us escape from, no matter what our job happens to be, and is reflected in the jigsaw at the beginning of this chapter. Each individual has to find his own answer to the jigsaw and what is virtually certain is that the pieces of the jigsaw, and their relative sizes will change with our progress through life. Initially, professional ambitions and pride may well dominate, and while there may be no time in any farmer's or farm manager's life when maximum profit or income is not an important objective, it is very likely that it will be an especially important driving force during the first half of anyone's career. Not suprisingly, however, the incentive to stretch oneself beyond a certain point and age, simply to increase income, can usually be expected to diminish. The hoary argument, however, that at this or any other stage, this makes farming primarily a way of life and not a business is a tedious irrelevance. Farming, of course, is both. So are most other businesses to those who manage and work in them and there is little point in farmers regarding their businesses as in some way different from those in the rest of the economy in this respect.

What is true for everybody, is that reconciling personal, domestic and family considerations with a desire to succeed professionally is an imprecise exercise. Setting objectives smacks of quantification and it is true that short and long term business plans can and should be quantified as far as possible. Management by objectives invites that approach. What is also true is that at the more personal level very little can or needs to be quantified in the same way. Finding the right blend between these two areas of his life is, however, an important part of any manager's life style. Inevitably there will be conflict. Inevitably the balance will change, at different times of his life. This adds to the frustrations involved in setting objectives. It is an uneven job. Parts of it can be quantified and parts cannot be, but it is a situation that must be recognised, thought about and lived with – not swept under the carpet.

One more area of conflict inherent in this subject is what might be called 'the carrot and the stick' effect. Initially, there can be certain comfort and encouragement from having cleared the decks and charted the course ahead. It is the sort of feeling that follows the preparation of next year's cropping plan or financial budget which are part and parcel of the wider task that we are talking about. Having stated that something is to be achieved almost creates the belief that it will be achieved. But we know better. For all kinds of reasons, some of them within our control and some of them beyond it, objectives are not always achieved. Indeed, in overall terms, they seldom are. Then the exercise may become more like a stick than a carrot. The comfort of having charted the way ahead changes to the discomfort of having committed oneself and having failed to keep to the chart. Too much disappointment over this should be avoided, as lessons can and should be learned. This topic will be returned to in Chapter 6, on control.

Finally, we should mention the question of time. The foregoing comments will have indicated that a serious consideration of objectives – using something like the approach of management by objectives – is not a simple task. It will therefore take time, over a period of time. It is commonly suggested that up to half a dozen sessions of several hours each will be required. That, in itself, will be a deterrent in a business like farming, where there is usually one manager, and the demands on his time are legion. It is even more of a deterrent when he realises that changing circumstances – changes in the external and internal environments, and changes in his own make-up and experience – will mean that before too long the whole job will have to be repeated. It is by no means a once-and-for-all task.

SUMMARY AND LIMITATIONS

This, then, is what setting objectives is about. It is a very important job, but it is a difficult one for a variety of reasons. It needs a careful assessment of the opportunities presented to a business by the external environment and an equally careful assessment of the possibilities that the internal resources offer. It requires self examination. It requires the help of others. It takes time and it will need repeating. But none of these are reasons for not doing it. On the contrary. While it may be important for managers to *do things well now in the short term*, it is equally important that they *think well for the long term*. There should be an emphasis here on the word 'well'. Success will not follow just because objectives have been set. It will follow if those objectives are good ones, and if they are then achieved.

In all of this, farmers and farm managers are in no sense different from managers in other sectors. When thinking about objectives, they are confronted by the same basic difficulties, and they have the same kinds of financial and personal needs. Each industry – not just farming – does, of course, have its own particular technical and commercial characteristics which need to be allowed for when objectives are being thought about and determined. The consequences of that exercise are what the rest of the book is largely about.

SOME QUESTIONS RELATING TO THIS CHAPTER

(1) Do you think it is possible to exercise control over your business without some clearly defined objectives?
(2) How often do you give serious consideration to the objectives of your business or job?
(3) How, precisely, do, or will, you set about determining your objectives, and who else might you involve in the process?
(4) Draw a jigsaw of your own professional and personal objectives.
(5) What are the key results areas in your business?
(6) Which of your present key results areas do you think are most likely to remain so in the foreseeable future, and which of them might not?

A GUIDE TO SELECTED FURTHER READING

Management by Objectives, 1970. Management Information Sheet no.14. London: British Institute of Management.
  A brief, itemised statement of what MBO is, what and who it involves, and what it requires in order for it to be successful.
Boyer, R. S. 1969. Management by Objectives. *Farm Management* **1**, no.5, 1–8.
  One of the few attempts to relate MBO specifically to farming situations.
Humble, J. W. 1972. *Improving Business Results*. London: McGraw-Hill; London: Pan Books.
  Described as, 'the definitive work' on MBO, but well within two evenings' pleasant reading. Interesting case-studies included.
Townsend, R. 1971. *Up the Organisation*. London: Hodder and Stoughton.
  Don't deny yourself the pleasure of reading this book. Worth having, if only for the section on Objectives – but for many other sections as well.

4
Planning

Planning involves making **time** available to determine:

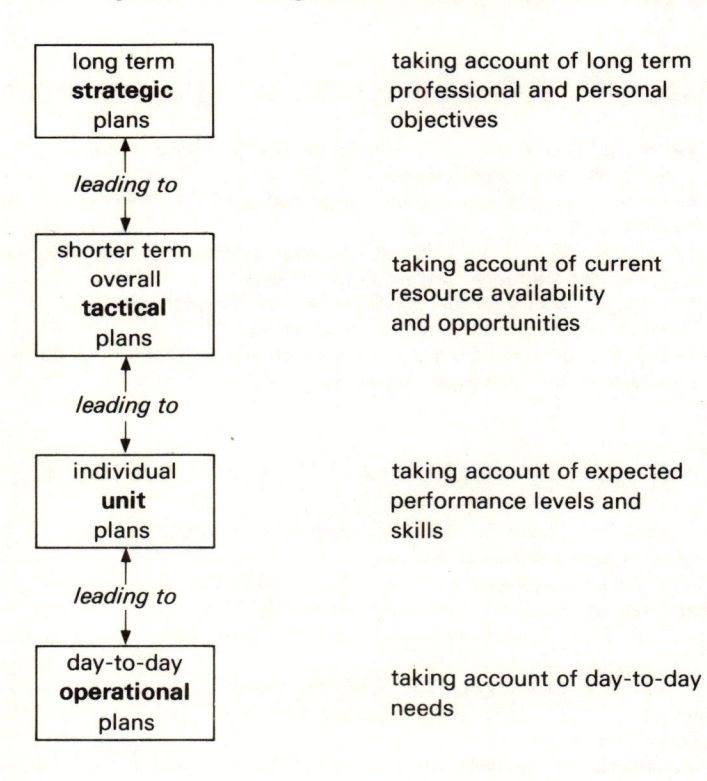

long term **strategic** plans	taking account of long term professional and personal objectives
leading to	
shorter term overall **tactical** plans	taking account of current resource availability and opportunities
leading to	
individual **unit** plans	taking account of expected performance levels and skills
leading to	
day-to-day **operational** plans	taking account of day-to-day needs

Some readers may feel that this chapter is inseparable from the previous one and in many respects they would be right. Some aspects of planning, such as drawing up long term strategic plans, follow on, with all the same internal and external constraints, from any consideration of overall goals and objectives. In this sense, planning, like the setting of objectives, is an integral part of overall management and not in any way a peripheral one. Success will not follow simply from objectives having been set. It will depend on how *good*, in the business sense of the word, those objectives prove to be, on how effectively they are subsequently translated into plans and, finally, on how well those plans are carried out.

We, therefore, see planning as closely related to objective setting, but separated from it. We also see the concept of planning as having several different connotations which need to be discussed. Therefore, it deserves this separate chapter, the first part of which examines the nature of planning and is followed by some examples of planning in farm situations.

THE NATURE OF PLANNING

First, we should be quite clear what we mean when we use the word 'plan'. It is commonly defined in dictionaries as, 'to arrange beforehand'. In other words it means to give time to something *before* it happens in order to have some influence over events *when* they happen. As managers, we should remember that. We wish to have some control over events, rather than to let events control us. It is unlikely that we will ever be completely successful in this aim but it is not an unreasonable one to have. Managers are, after all, supposed to manage. Too often we may say that we *plan* to do something when what is really meant is that we *intend* to do it. The real meaning of planning is worth remembering. It requires that time should be given to events before they happen. It is the principal way in which the careful manager avoids what is popularly known as, 'management by crisis' – the situations in which managers spend their time and energies responding to things that have gone wrong. By contrast, managers who spend time planning, try to anticipate difficulties and mistakes – and certainly to learn from them when they occur – so that future events are less stressful and more successful.

There are several other important characteristics of planning which need emphasis. First, it should not be thought that planning relates solely – or even primarily – to the production process in its limited technical sense. In farm management circles it has tended to be the case that planning has in fact become synonymous with farm planning, i.e. with choosing a combination of enterprises. This is unfortunate, although it is true that most of the recognisable planning techniques have been applied to this aspect of farm management. However, remembering our definition of planning – to arrange beforehand – it will be obvious to the reader that the process is important across the whole range of management problems. It may be just as important to spend time planning such matters as the cash flow for the next six months, or the recruitment of a new member of staff, or the marketing of some particular commodity, as it is to spend time on *the farm cropping plan*. Indeed, important as the farm plan undoubtedly is, there are many other aspects of management, similar to those just mentioned, that will need more constant attention, at less predictable intervals than will the farm plan, if management by crisis is really to be avoided.

Planning is not only necessary across a wide range of management issues, but also across a wide range of time horizons. As already noted, plans may be closely related to long term objective setting, making use of well established methods of financial budgeting. Plans of this kind may stretch tentatively ahead for several years, spelling out the approximate path to be followed, or, in much more detail, they may relate to the immediate farming year ahead. But, just as importantly, they may relate to a specific operation or innovation such as the installation of a new piece of machinery or the introduction into the system of a new enterprise. Or again, plans may relate to some routine farming operation, such as the annual harvest, or simply to a day's work for an individual, involving perhaps a collection of different jobs all of which need to be completed and must be fitted into a limited period of time. In our experience a little time spent towards the end of each day planning the next one, or towards the end of each week, month or season, planning the next one, can be time well spent. Having the peace of mind that stems from a plan helps to allow flexibility with which to cope with unforeseen events.

It follows from this discussion that planning is *not* synonymous with production planning nor with sophisticated planning techniques. Such techniques are sometimes needed and can be used with advantage, especially in the production and financial sectors of management. They will be referred to again in the chapters dealing with those topics. It will be clear, however, from the range of management situations mentioned here, and which at some time or another require a planning input, that what is needed may often be no more than an ordered consideration of the facts and possibilities involved. We believe that everyday human attributes such as thoroughness, orderliness and that indefinable thing called 'judgement' will usually play a major part in the process.

Two other important aspects of planning should be mentioned. First, there are many situations in which managers will not find themselves planning from scratch. Plans, however derived, usually already exist; cropping programmes are in being; labour forces exist; capital has already been invested. More often than not, therefore, plans relate to changes and adjustments to existing plans and the scope for adjustment will be constrained by what already exists. It would be attractive if we could always start with a clean slate, but that is seldom the case. This explains why, of all the existing financial planning tools, the partial budget – designed to assess the effect of change – is still the most frequently needed and used.

Secondly, if there is one fact that is common to most plans, it is that, probably, they will not work out exactly as they were planned. The failure of a plan in this sense may or may not matter depending on the particular circumstances. What does matter is that the reasons for failures are understood and that lessons for the future are learned. In this sense a failed plan can sometimes teach us more than when things work out entirely as expected. Furthermore, the failure of some plans is certainly not an argument for not planning or budgeting. All planning is, by definition, about future events. When we plan we are trying either to *predict* or to *arrange* what will happen in the future. But we cannot *know* what will happen in the future. In the financial context this is especially true during periods of rapidly changing prices and costs. Past trends and current levels then become a less reliable guide to the future and there may be a strong temptation not to plan, not to budget and perhaps not to change anything. This could be a mistake. It can be argued that it is *because* of uncertainty that planning is necessary and that increased uncertainty calls for more planning rather than less. There are, anyhow, those elements in planning – the physical ones – which become neither easier nor more difficult to predict because of uncertain financial circumstances. It should also be remembered that it is in fact impossible, in any situation, literally to do nothing. To do nothing is to do something. It is to go on doing what you have been doing; to commit your *present* plans and policies to *tomorrow's* (unknown) prices and costs. Profits, in fact, are the reward for accepting the risks that accompany uncertainty and careful planning is one way in which managers learn to respond to uncertainty. Caution there may need to be, but it could be dangerous to become so mesmerised by uncertainty as to reject all possibility of change.

It will be appreciated from what has been written so far in this chapter that planning is a wide-ranging concept. There are many different aspects of managing a farm business, embracing differing time horizons, which demand planning. It will call for care and it will often not be easy. On both of these counts it will, therefore, require time. Such evidence as exists on how United Kingdom farmers and farm managers spend their time suggests that planning tends to receive relatively little of it; on average, but obviously depending on the size and nature of the business, about 8%. We would be surprised if the situation was vastly different in other countries. We would agree that forward planning should not become so important as to undermine the need to do today's job well; the future, indeed, may depend on that. But it must also depend on an intelligent anticipation of future events. That is what planning is about.

There now follows examples of how planning can be used in each of the four main sectors of a business that we have identified: production, marketing, financing and staffing. These examples are of actual farming situations known to us. They have not been presented in order to demonstrate the detailed working out of plans, and certainly not to provide precise answers to the particular situations. They are intended to demonstrate simply the broad spectrum across which planning is necessary and the kinds of consideration that must be incorporated into that process.

PLANNING PRODUCTION ON THE FARM

The introduction of an acreage of broad beans to extend a group pea-vining enterprise is used to demonstrate the many and widely differing aspects involved in the planning of production on the farm.

In this particular case, a number of producers of peas for the canning trade operate, on a co-operative basis, the necessary equipment for cutting and vining together with transport vehicles to deliver their crop to a nearby processing factory. Faced with the escalating annual cost of operation, they need to give consideration to possible ways of extending the acreage covered, thus spreading the considerable overhead proportion of these costs.

A wide range of soil types, planting dates and varieties are used to extend the pea harvesting season to the limit of some five to six weeks. The viners operate for approximately 12 hours per day, but round the clock harvesting is out of the question, due to limited capacity of the factory canning lines. The offer of a contract to grow an area of broad beans which are harvested after the peas would seem to be an attractive proposition. Using the contract price and average yield data for the district, gross margin figures are shown to be similar to those for peas. Apart from changing sieves on the viners the harvesting machinery required for the two crops is identical.

There are, however, many implications in the growing and harvesting of broad beans which, if the enterprise is to be successful, need to receive considerable planning, e.g.:

(a) Loss of alternative crop. The introduction of a bean acreage with unproven returns will naturally replace an existing crop which has a known performance on the farm. A partial budget can be used in this situation to indicate the most likely beneficial change.
(b) Soil type and field selection. Rotational considerations may become a problem if the area of the farm currently devoted to peas and beans is already approaching 20%. Suitable fields for vining beans will need to be well drained, free from steep slopes, clean, fertile and preferably slightly heavier in texture than for peas or well manured to help the moisture retaining capacity.
(c) Competition for labour. On predominantly arable farms

where the majority of vining peas tend to be grown, apart from late spraying and the harvesting of winter barley it is possible to supply staff to the vining operation without too much difficulty. Extension of vining into August with the beans will, in most years, cause serious competition with the harvesting of spring barley, herbage seeds and oil seed rape. It is not just the numbers of people required but the fact that the skilled staff needed to drive the combines are also the viner operators.

(d) Drilling machines. Although peas are drilled with a standard type corn drill, one commonly used variety of bean, triple white, is larger, flat-sided and therefore needs to be planted with a specialised machine. There is also the need to drill the crop in rows sufficiently wide to enable hand rouging, so that planting is slower than with peas and costs are markedly increased.

(e) Pests and diseases. Although the need to control aphids will be increased with a bean acreage, few additional crop health problems should be experienced and no additional machinery will be required.

(f) Rouging. This is an additional task essential to the growing of broad beans for the canning market. Rouge plants produce beans which in the cooking process following canning, turn black and are unacceptable to the market. The growing crop has therefore to be rouged with care on two or three occasions during and after flowering. This will usually need to take place in the month of June and will therefore compete with other arable tasks. It is a laborious process but with efficient short term planning can be fitted into part-days along with other more weather-dependent jobs such as spraying or hay making.

(g) Staff morale. The operators of cutting and vining machinery find that after several weeks' involvement, they begin to lose motivation. Long working days with travelling to other farms in the group, often some distance from home, are naturally tiring. The driving of harvesting machinery involves considerable concentration, often in difficult weather conditions from hot to wet and muddy, and noise is also a problem especially to viner drivers. Extension of the vining season will therefore require important planning of the labour force. Weekly or fortnightly shifts may be a possibility but however

dealt with, it is vital to maintain the morale of the field staff throughout the vining season.
(h) Field management input. Another aspect which, although at the end of the list, is the important one of field organisation and supervision. Efficient operation of the whole process necessitates a continuous input of management, not only to co-ordinate activity in the field but also to liaise at all times with the factory. Although the same machines are used for harvesting the two crops, more attention is required to the wilting of beans prior to optimum vining and to the regular delivery of 'warm' beans to the factory.

Each of the issues listed needs to be thought about thoroughly to avoid crisis and disruption of other activities on the farms concerned.

FINANCIAL PLANNING ON THE FARM

The farm business requires a continuing input of management on the financial side, but especially at a time of major capital injection. An arable farmer was convinced by experience that break crops were essential to the achievement of high cereal yields on his farm. He was growing herbage seeds and oil seed rape but although both crops required minimal additional capital for harvesting and storage, they were producing a somewhat variable financial return.

Changes to the farming system were considered in order to intensify production and achieve one of the major objectives of the business, i.e. to enable a son to come into the business. A beef fattening enterprise was therefore planned to utilise forage maize and conserved grass, but as no suitable buildings were available, major capital spending was required.

Store cattle would be purchased in the autumn, selling to slaughter during the late winter and early spring. In addition to the cattle building, silage clamps, handling and weighing area, harvesting and feeding machinery were also required.

Estimating likely profitability from such an enterprise did not prove to be easy, but the importance of technical efficiency in converting forages into beef clearly showed to be a key factor. The return on the investment in fixed equipment would not be high, but as the farm was owned, the building would add to the longer term value of the farm. It was, in fact, designed so that conversion to dairy cattle housing would be a future possibility.

Some capital was available for the project but considerable borrowing would be required, especially to cover the working capital for stock and feed. The bank was to be approached for overdraft facilities and so detailed planning of the financial aspects was also essential. Cash flows had first to be calculated for the existing enterprises, taking into account loss of crops being replaced by forages. Payments for the buildings, facilities and equipment were then taken into account, as well as grant receipts. The estimated cost of store cattle, purchased feed and sale receipts were also incorporated so that an overall cash picture was available.

It was at this stage that alternative actions could be considered to even out undue peak requirements for borrowing. Forward sales of cereals were an obvious possibility as was earlier depopulation of the building in the spring by selling the remaining cattle back into the store market rather than waiting for them to fatten. Hiring of harvesting machinery or the use of a contractor was considered in order to minimise the need for capital. The latter was ruled out due to timeliness of harvesting being a major factor determining silage quality.

PLANNING MARKETING ON THE FARM

The production of beef from young bulls is an example of a farm enterprise where the financial returns are very much dependent upon the establishment and maintenance of a satisfactory market outlet for the product. Traditionally in the UK, the only bulls processed by the meat trade have been used for breeding purposes and have therefore produced carcasses with a tendency to be tough, dark-coloured and often with an unacceptable taint. The producers of bull beef from young, intensively fed animals had therefore a difficult initial task proving to the buyers that their product was very different and that it really did meet modern customer requirements.

The advantages to the producer of leaving his cattle entire are largely in terms of improved growth rate and feed conversion efficiency. In addition, he should expect a premium price as the carcasses produce a higher proportion of saleable meat than is obtained from steers. The product is lean and tender but is usually slightly darker in colour than steer or heifer beef.

Problems can arise in production, transportation and at the abattoirs which lead to excess leaness or dark flesh and rejection by the butcher. Planning is, therefore, essential at all stages in order to ensure an acceptable product, but one which also justifies a premium price.

Long term planning

As soon as a retail outlet has satisfactorily introduced bull beef to its customers continuity of supply is of paramount importance. It is harmful to sales to have to change back for short periods to a product with a somewhat different appearance. Communications between the buyer and individual or groups of producers are, therefore, essential in order to plan long term supplies. Regular numbers will at times be difficult to provide but an expanding requirement is even more difficult to match as this requires the inputs into production being critically timed.

Short term planning

The problem of dark-coloured meat is made worse by allowing the bulls to get excited during selection and drafting out of the housing, in transportation and particularly at the abattoirs. Careful planning of all these processes is, therefore, necessary and for initial deliveries it is advantageous for the farmer or stockman to travel with the consignment in order to ensure careful handling at every stage.

On arrival at the abattoirs the bulls should be moved direct to the slaughtering area and not put into lairage where they may come within sight or smell of female cattle. Individual animals within a production group often prove difficult to 'finish', i.e. continue to grow and do not develop sufficient flesh or fatty tissue to produce an acceptable carcass. Such animals need to be sold separately as culls and not allowed to spoil the image of prime quality bull beef.

PLANNING EMPLOYMENT ON THE FARM

Some two years after taking over the management of a large, predominantly arable, downland farm, the manager wished to expand the livestock enterprises. These comprised a flock of 300 half-bred ewes and a herd of 80 outdoor sows, producing weaners for sale. Both enterprises were performing well, due in no small way to a first class stockman ably assisted by a recently qualified student and with occasional help from tractor drivers at busy periods such as lambing. The senior stockman, when given the choice, did prefer to work with sheep and he certainly had the capability to handle a much larger flock. In order to expand the sow herd it would be necessary to recruit a skilled pigman ideally experienced in the rigorous environment of outdoor farrowing. The problem immediately arose that all the farm cottages were occupied, and the job to be filled was unsuited to a single person who could possibly be found accommodation in the district. This planning exercise, instigated to consider employing a pigman, developed to a stage where major reorganisation of the farming system occurred. Several members of staff took on new duties, no additional person was, in fact, employed and the output and profitability of the farm increased markedly.

The two farming years although somewhat contrasting in weather patterns, had clearly pinpointed to the manager the strengths and weaknesses of the existing farming system. Arable crops comprised cereals, sugar beet and potatoes, the root crops being grown on the deeper soils in the lower areas of the farm. Yields of winter cereals were most encouraging especially when drilled early; a situation difficult to achieve with all the acreage due to the competing tasks of harvesting the beet and potatoes. Financial performance of both root crops was unsatisfactory, and the machinery was aged and 'written-off'. The soils were far from ideal, the beet factory 90 miles distant and storage facilities for potatoes somewhat limited.

Replacement of the roots by cereals and additional ley for sheep and pigs would maintain a satisfactory rotation and at the same time reduce the autumn peak labour requirement. Such a change of cropping would release a tractor driver and of the three employed, the younger man was the one who regularly volunteered to assist the stockmen and noticeably had a 'way' with stock. He had, in fact, spent time working with cattle in his first farm job and after several years in the seat of a tractor, was keen to take on the challenge of becoming a skilled pigman. He and his family were happy in their cottage, settled into village life and therefore preferring not to move away. The job was offered to him and he readily accepted.

Other considerations which were taken into account in planning the changes were:

(a) The present stockmen were consulted and in full agreement with the suggestions. Although the present head stockman would become virtually a full time shepherd he would be available to give help and advice on the pig side, in fact they would regularly assist each other at busy times.
(b) There would be a delay in the purchase of additional ewes until several months after the discontinuation of root growing to enable leys to be established and allow time for the new man to work with the others and learn the necessary skills.
(c) Attendance at short term courses was arranged for such aspects as animal health and nutrition which could be far better learned from professional teachers than from his colleagues on the farm.
(d) Pig records. The expanding herd would need to have a more comprehensive set of physical and financial records and the new man was inducted into the expanded system by the manager himself.
(e) Careful consideration had to be given to remuneration of the staff in their new roles. Additional payments were justified by people taking on additional responsibility, so avoiding the likelihood of causing ill feeling with other members of the staff who may have considered that they had been overlooked for promotion.

SOME QUESTIONS RELATING TO THIS CHAPTER

(1) Planning is about the future. The future is unknown, so why bother to plan?
(2) Do you have an overall financial plan (budget) for your business for the current year? If not, why not?
(3) What proportion of your time do you spend planning?
(4) Do you set out plans each day, week, month?
Has it helped, or would it help you to do so?

(5) How important are the skills of individual staff members when formulating an overall labour plan?
(6) 'Planning is less important on a small farm.' Do you agree?

A GUIDE TO SELECTED FURTHER READING

Barnard, C. S. and J. S. Nix 1973. *Farm Planning and Control.* Cambridge: Cambridge University Press.
Chapter 1 (The planning environment and the managerial function) is valuable reading in its own right but is essential for those who intend to get more involved in this basic text.

Nix, J. S. 1969. Annotated bibliography of farm planning and programming techniques. *Farm Management* **1,** no.7.
Could save you a lot of unnecessary reading or researching.

Drucker, P. F. 1967. *Managing for Results.* London: Heinemann; London: Pan Books.
Chapter 11 (Making the future today) is salutary comment on a preoccupation with 'tomorrow'.

Humble, J. W. 1972. *Improving Business Results.* London: Pan Books.
Already recommended for the previous chapter, but Part Two is relevant here also.

5
Decision making

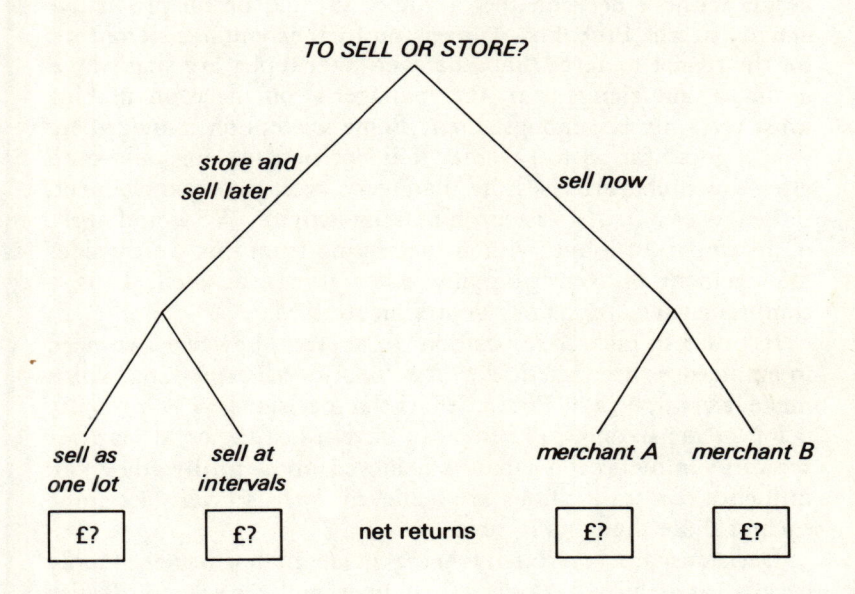

```
                TO SELL OR STORE?
               /                 \
        store and              sell now
        sell later
         /      \              /        \
    sell as   sell at      merchant A   merchant B
    one lot   intervals
     [£?]     [£?]    net returns  [£?]    [£?]
```

Decision making has many facets. It may concern the present or the future; it may concern a trivial or a major issue; and the available options may be few or many, quantifiable or not quantifiable. Whatever the circumstances, however, decisions usually have to be taken *now*, based in part at least, on information that comes from the *past*, about events that will happen at some time in the *future*. Seen in that light, it is seldom an entirely easy process and when management was once described as the art of making good decisions based on inadequate information, it came close to the truth.

THE IMPORTANCE OF DECISION MAKING

Once again, in discussing this topic, we come face to face with the inter-relationships between different aspects of management. As we have seen, it is vital to have clear objectives, to devise plans which reflect those objectives and, as we shall see in the next chapter, to try to ensure that things happen as planned. Planning and controlling are linked by the fact that managers take decisions; decisions to do certain things in certain ways. Events actually occur because managers decide that they should occur; without decision there would, in fact, be no productive activity at all. Probably, it needs no further emphasis from us, for the reader to agree that whatever other topics are singled out as important elements in the manager's job, decision making must certainly be amongst them. Some writers on management would go so far as to say that it is decision making, above all else, which characterises the manager's role; that management, in fact, is *essentially* a decision making activity. We would agree on its importance but, without detracting from this we consider management to concern many other things as well. It is a comprehensive task as our definition stressed.

In order to make our position quite clear, however, we need to emphasise three particular aspects of decision making which make it so important. First, the fact that decisions are *continually* being made; second, that they can have a lasting, or at least *far reaching* influence on what is achieved and, thirdly, they can influence *how well* things are achieved. Let us briefly examine each of these thoughts in turn.

Decisions are continually being made in businesses if only because something is continually happening. It is easy to identify decision making with change, with a shift of emphasis or methods. What is equally true is that if events continue unaltered, it is because a decision has been made (albeit automatically or subconsciously) not to change. It is unlikely that the manager of a dairy farm, for instance, consciously decides to go on milking his cows each day, but in effect, each day that he does go on milking them he is allowing capital, labour and management to be employed in this particular way. A considered intention to do nothing is, therefore, to take a positive action; it is to commit present day resources and plans to tomorrow's prices and costs. Financial outcomes are thus being determined by decisions not to change – or to change – as the case may be, and decision making, in this sense, becomes a continuous part of management.

Turning to the second point that we wish to make here, it is important to be aware of those situations when decisions are being made that will have a far-reaching effect on the future course of a farm business, and, at those times, to leave no stone unturned in an endeavour to make good decisions. No more can be expected. There is hardly such a concept as a *right* decision. Only the outcome of the *chosen* course of action is ever known. Other possible outcomes – which may have been better, or worse – are never known. *Good* strategic decisions are, therefore, what are sought, compatible with long term objectives and with the constraints and possibilities that should have been built into those objectives. From time to time decisions to abandon an enterprise, to introduce another, or to expand or contract – perhaps even to change farms – will need to be made. They may influence the course of a business and the rewards from it for years ahead; they should not be taken lightly.

Our third point is simply that *how* enterprises are managed (as opposed to *what* enterprises are managed) will also have a very important influence on what results are achieved. The significance of technical competence has already been mentioned in an earlier chapter and will be mentioned again in later ones. It cannot be over-stressed. Many day-to-day and week-to-week decisions will have to be made, often in the face of changing weather conditions that certainly do complicate the farm manager's life in a way that they don't for many of his counterparts in other parts of the economy. These are the tactical decisions. They must always be made in the context of longer term strategic decisions that will, hopefully, already have been taken. In the long term they will have less significance than strategic decisions about *what* to do, but in the context of a particular crop, a particular season and a particular year's profit, they can be vital. And perhaps what should be added here – not just as an afterthought – is that more often than not such decisions will not relate to a *problem* as such. It will simply be that a decision between one possible course of action and another, or between several possibilities, has to be taken. Indeed, the need for decision making at all, comes about only because there is a choice between alternatives. Without that choice there is no need for decision, and whilst Drucker reminds us of the dangers of seeking the right answer to the wrong question, it may be even more helpful not, automatically, to identify *decision making* with *problem solving*, but simply with *selecting* between alternatives: alternative issues or courses of action rather than problems as such.

THE COMPONENTS OF DECISION MAKING

So far we have written in fairly general terms about the importance of decision making, but what, in fact, does it involve? In this section we try to answer that question by identifying those procedures which a manager should – mentally at least – engage in if he is to take his decision making seriously. We are not suggesting that in every situation and wherever a choice of any kind has to be made by a farmer or farm manager, he will, or should, go through this formal and apparently laborious process. That would be tedious and, depending on the issue in hand, often unnecessary. Nevertheless, the sequence of thinking that is set out below is probably more often required than not and, again depending on the issue in hand, could be dangerous to by-pass.

(1) *Identify the issue or problem in hand*

This may seem so obvious as not to require mention, but we do *not* want to spend valuable time finding the right answer to the wrong problem, with all the wastefulness of effort and resources which that implies. It is all too easy, however, for any of us to be guilty of 'symptomatic diagnosis', as the jargon describes it; clutching at first impressions and failing, perhaps, to go back to 'square one' questions.

(2) *Assessing significance*

With the first hurdle overcome, it is important for a busy manager – and what manager is not busy? – to assess the significance of the issue that he has now identified and to which he is addressing himself. How important is this issue in terms of capital commitment, profit potential, morale of staff, influence on other activities and possibilities, and how irreversible would a wrong decision in this area prove to be? In short, how much time does it deserve and whose time, within the business, does it deserve?

Managers must constantly be prepared to determine priorities, a topic we shall consider later in the book. Considering significance, in this way, will help a manager to allocate his efforts appropriately and determine how formal he needs to be in reaching a decision in the area in question.

(3) *Considering alternatives*

Assuming that the issue has been identified and has been judged to be significant, a careful consideration of the possible alternative courses of action should now be embarked on. At this stage it is important to keep an open mind; to consult and discuss as widely as possible – inside and outside the business – and not to 'close the book' too hastily. Initially many alternatives will be healthier than few; discussion and reflection will then serve to narrow down the real possibilites.

(4) *Collecting information*

This will be an essential part of the operation. What is wanted will be partly determined by the kind of evaluation that is subsequently envisaged. All of the normal rules about budgeting will apply; reliable physical data allied to the best possible estimates of future prices and costs is needed; muster all the accuracy that you possibly can. The task will not be easy, especially if activities are being contemplated that are new to the business concerned. If that is the case, it must be remembered that case study and experimental data can be a poor guide to commercial operation on *your* farm under *your* management. Remember also that 'over the fence' impressions and verbal accounts of results from neighbours and associates can – with no intent to mislead – be less than the whole truth. Real communication at this level can be elusive. It is also important, even in situations where quantitative evaluation is possible, that non-quantitative information should also be sought. The effect of possible changes in patterns of production on such matters as ease of organisation, personal strain, and quality control may be important considerations. Getting reliable facts, before they become part of your own history, requires careful research and we devote Chapter 12 to it.

(5) *Evaluation*

Not all decision making situations will lead to the point where numerical evaluation is necessary, although, by definition, some judgement will always be required in the light of the issue in hand, the options that are open and whatever information about those options can be gleaned. Where, however, numerical evaluation is both indicated and possible, it is our firm belief that the time-honoured partial budget (what *extra* income and cost and what *avoided* income and cost is involved?) is the most simple, effective and, therefore, appropriate management tool to use. Managers would be well advised to become adept in its use. The partial budget is essentially concerned with *changes* in profitability and will need to be interpreted in the light of other non-numerical considerations. Where investment is involved – and some capital appraisal is required – the partial budget can, without undue complications, lead on to a simple calculation of the percentage return of the extra profit on the amount of fresh capital required to generate it. This is known, simply, as the rate of return, or alternatively, (omitting any depreciation element from the budget) an estimate can be made of how quickly the investment will be recouped, the 'pay back' method as it is known. With outside help of a specialist kind, more sophisticated evaluation methods and operational research techniques may be of guidance, but we believe that, for many cases, the simple approach, applied by the manager himself, has advantages. Some of these approaches will be returned to again in more detail in other chapters, and the recommended chapters in the two farm management books listed at the end of this chapter provide good guidance in their use.

(6) *Choice*

Sooner or later (depending on the scale and type of problem or issue) there will come the moment of decision. A choice – if it is a decision situation at all – will have to be made, even if it is to do nothing. Very often the actual moment of decision may be difficult to recognise; a concensus of opinion tends to develop in the face of evidence – some economic and some not – so that a good decision emerges. This will usually suggest that sound preliminary work has been done at the sifting and evaluation stage. Time and facts have eliminated the non-starters. At other times there will be more agony. Non-quantitative considerations then, perhaps, become more important. Judgement and experience take over from calculations and some managers, of course, become more adept in these matters than others.

(7) *Implementation*

A decision taken, must then be acted upon; the decision must be properly communicated to those responsible for its implementation. It may be a simple internal matter involving one or more persons, or a major development involving professional and commercial interests outside the farm business. Sequencing of events will then become important and we are right back into the realms of planning.

(8) *Checking results*

Decisions are taken because certain desired results are anticipated. They may not always occur. What happens as a result of a decision should be monitored – numerically or otherwise – and checked against expectations. Faults should be corrected as quickly as possible before events drift permanently off track. But now we are into another major realm of business, namely, that of control.

(9) *Responsibility*

Finally, whether a decision proves to have been a good one or not, management must be prepared to take responsibility for it. Hopefully, appropriate consultation within an organisation will have taken place at all stages. Decisions may or may not have emerged by mutual agreement and concensus, but responsibility for the final moment or act of decision and its implementation rests fairly and squarely with management. That is one of the things that managers are paid for. If a good decision has been made they can enjoy the knowledge that they inspired it; if it has not, they shoulder the blame – if that is the right word.

THE IMPORTANCE OF JUDGEMENT AND TIME

Before going on to illustrate the application of this systematic approach to decision making we wish to say a final word, on the importance of 'judgement' and of 'time' in the context of this chapter. It will have been clear to the reader that although numerical techniques can play an important part in the overall process that has just been described – especially in items (2) to (5) dealing with alternative courses of action and their evaluation – there are other aspects of the process which rely very much more on subjective assessment using experience and judgement. In our estimation, judgement is an important quality in all aspects of management. Although not easy to define it is a word that we wish to stress. In the decision making process it is especially important in items (1) and (6), i.e. in recognising the issue and in selecting the preferred course of action. It is at the all important beginning and end of the process that the ability to exercise judgement plays its part; preparing the way for evaluation and interpreting the results of it.

We believe that closely related to a manager's ability to exercise judgement is his ability to recognise when a particular matter deserves his time, and his willingness to give it. Often during the course of the working day or week quick decisions are needed in the interest of everybody and everything involved. Good managers will learn when such decisions can safely be made and when they cannot be. As a general rule, hasty decisions should not be made in the strategic situations referred to earlier, especially when significant amounts of capital are involved, or when, for any other reason, including the safety of employees, situations are not easily reversible. It is in those situations in particular that it is important for managers to give, without unnecessary delay, that amount of time to decision making which leaves them, at the conclusion, as confident as they can be that their decision has been a good one – and may even have been the right one.

EXAMPLE OF A STRATEGIC DECISION

The decision to introduce a system of **complete diet feeding** (CDF) to a dairy herd is taken to illustrate a complex decision, involving not only the feeding of cows but also the management and organisation of a dairy enterprise. The system involves mixing forages, concentrates and other constituents of a diet in a specialised mixer-feeder trailer which is fitted with a weighing mechanism; the ration then being dispensed to a group of cows which has constant access to the manger except at milking times. Feeding during milking is eliminated, and intake of an individual cow is determined by her appetite and by management decisions as to which group she belongs to and the composition of the diets. There are many physical, nutritional and financial considerations to be taken into account before making a decision to introduce CDF but a systematic approach can be seen to be of value.

(1) *Identify the issue*

This system of feeding dairy cattle can be looked upon as being applicable only to a large herd situation where high yields and margins are being achieved. The capital cost of the mixer-feeder alone is a considerable sum but if building modifications are necessary to store ingredients or to provide mangers then herd performance is of major importance. There is no magic associated with the machine, as the diets produced are only as good as the ingredients used, so that if a dairy farmer is unsatisfied with the current herd performance, he should identify and correct any shortcomings before contemplating CDF. Key factors in the profitability of dairy farming include the availability of high quality forages together with skilled and dedicated herdsmanship. These factors are also essential to successful CDF and the system can be best looked upon as one which can help the 'good' to become even 'better'.

(2) *Assessing significance*

The majority of high performance dairy units have, in recent years, undergone a logical sequence of changes in the way in which cows have been fed and managed. Self-feeding of silage has been replaced by mechanical handling of precision-chopped material fed in mangers. As well as feeding concentrates at milking time, one or more additional feeds have been introduced outside the parlour to spread intake, and help rumen digestion. To a dairy farmer who has followed this pattern of development, CDF is the next logical step. He will need only to replace the normal forage box with a mixer-feeder and will also avoid the cost of parlour feeders as and when they need replacement. He will need to assess at this stage, the effect of the system on his staff in terms of skills, training and motivation.

(3) *Considering alternatives*

There are several feasible alternative systems of feeding a large high-yielding herd which justify serious consideration:

(a) Mixing complete diets without the purchase of a specialised machine, by adding food ingredients in layers into a forage box or converted manure spreader. These machines take longer to fill, they do not usually have a weighing device and the standard of mix is less satisfactory.
(b) Feeding of forages and concentrates as normal at milking time but providing additional concentrates from cow-activated automatic dispensers located in the housing areas. Development of these units continues but as the level of sophistication increases so does the cost to a sum equal or in excess of CDF machinery. One major snag of these feeders, that has been pinpointed by behavioural studies, is the wide variability of use by individual cows within the herd.
(c) Automatic dispensing of concentrates from a timed augering device, to every cow in the front of the cubicles. This system, although considerably more expensive in initial cost and in maintenance, requires a low labour input. It is a possible alternative in a building layout which does not provide satisfactory space for mangers or access for feeding vehicles.

(4) *Collecting information*

We have indicated in the early part of this chapter that this is often an important factor in decision making and it is especially so with this example. Although a few machines have been operating in the UK for several years, widespread interest in CDF is more recent, so that minimal research and development work has been justified. Many trials are now in progress but it will be some time before input : output data is available for various diets, breeds, machines or other such variables. The feeding of a dairy cow is also a long term consideration; a change in nutrition may well affect milk output in the short term, but it also has a longer term effect upon milk quality, cow weight, condition and conception rate. The common practice in farming to ask a neighbour how he is getting on with his new machine, is not always the ideal way to obtain an unbiased opinion. It is only natural for a person who has made the decision to spend a large capital sum to see more clearly the advantages and to be hopeful that any snags are of a temporary nature. Fortunately, not all farmers react in this way and reliable information can be obtained from users often through contacts such as ADAS machinery advisers. These users will detail the problems they have experienced in such matters as cows being unwilling to come into the parlour, a percentage of animals which on ad-lib feed put on flesh and fat rather than produce milk. The question of summer feeding will arise, including the possibility of CDF throughout the year or using the machine to buffer grazing with other types of feed.

(5) *Evaluation*

Numerical evaluation should be possible with this example at least as far as putting a sum to the additional costs that CDF will involve. The capital requirement will be known, so that taking depreciation, interest, maintenance and repairs, an annual charge can be calculated. Labour costs will seldom be included in the calculation as a change to CDF should not alter the number of staff employed, although in some situations overtime payments may be affected. Cost per animal will be markedly reduced if the machinery can also be used to service a heifer-rearing or a beef unit on the same farm. Several dairy herds could also be fed using one machine if travelling distance was reasonable or where manger capacity allowed alternate day filling. Turning to the calculation of the benefits, this is a more difficult area, but one which will become less so as the results of current trials become available. Some savings in cost may well be obtained, e.g. the price of concentrates bulk-tipped compared to the same material blown into hoppers above a parlour or obtained in sacks for the 'out of parlour' feeds. Purchased proprietary concentrates can be replaced by using the machine as a 'home-mixer' and buying ingredients on a least-cost basis. Deducting such savings from the additional costs will leave a sum to be covered by increased output, i.e. to show a break even situation. Some managers may, in a period of marked inflation, be satisfied with such a situation coupled with the expectation of having a system easier for staff to operate and one which can be more satisfactorily controlled from the farm office. Others will require a certain return on the investment and will therefore need to calculate the additional returns required. The difficulty arises in putting a value not just on any additional milk output but also on such factors as improved conception rate and change in calving pattern.

(6) *Choice*

Having followed the factors through in detail to this stage, it should be a relatively clear-cut decision as to whether the system in a particular situation is justified or not. If alternative feeding systems became more attractive in the future, the mixer-feeder trailer could be used as a simple forage dispenser.

(7) *Implementation*

The successful outcome of the new system is very much dependent upon the way it is implemented so that several important tasks follow:

(a) Explain in detail to all staff the likely benefits, but more importantly the expected difficulties. The difficulty of cows entering the parlour could develop into a major problem or be considered as a challenge depending upon the level of motivation in the stockmen.
(b) Arrange a training session for the operators – to be undertaken by the local dealers or manufacturers' staff.
(c) Assemble a supply of appropriate spare parts and make arrangements with the dealer and perhaps in conjunction with other local users, to ensure availability of an emergency parts service.
(d) Prepare a system of information flow from office to feeder and back to enable accurate control.
(e) Introduce the diets to the cows over an extended period so as to avoid digestive upset especially with the high yielding groups.

(8) *Checking Results*

As well as recording feed dispensed on a daily basis, monthly or even weekly stock checks will be necessary to enable inputs to the herd as a whole to be compared with budgeted figures. Accuracy of feeding to the various groups will depend upon the weighing mechanism of the mixer-feeder so that a periodic check over a weighbridge is a valuable operation. Milk output from each group can be obtained by taking bulk tank dipstick readings between groups or ideally from an in-line flow meter. Cow weights and condition scores will be a useful indicator to the longer term benefits of the new system.

(9) *Responsibility*

It follows from the previous point that a manager making a decision to introduce CDF may well have to go through a difficult period when the problems are obvious to all but the benefits much less so. Motivation of the stockmen will be a major factor through this period, but if careful implementation is carried out as outlined, few difficulties should arise. This is, in fact, the job of management – to take the decisions, and to take the responsibility for them which involves seeing them through to fruition.

EXAMPLE OF A TACTICAL DECISION

Managers involved in making a strategic decision, as in the previous example, have adequate time in which to carefully consider all the various aspects, but especially to obtain relevant information. Many other farm management decisions and often equally important ones in terms of financial outcome, have to be made in a much shorter period of time. Tactical decisions are taken on a daily basis, such as when to cut a ley for hay, or they may be 'one-off' decisions dealing with a crisis or unexpected problem. Take, for example, a potato grower who is finding difficulty during an unusually wet harvest in obtaining sufficient pickers to lift his crop. He has in recent years tried a mechanical harvester but found that hand pickers cause less tuber damage to the variety, Record, of which he grows a considerable acreage for a crisping contract. With such a high value crop (a figure which can be estimated with reasonable accuracy) still in the ground and one which is beginning to deteriorate, a quick solution has to be found. Despite the urgency, there is much to be gained from thinking the problem through, using the logical sequence that we have suggested. Not all the factors are now as relevant but some certainly are e.g.:

(1) *Identify the problem*

This is not the time to be considering the long term situation regarding potatoes on the farm. Recovering the crop still in the ground as soon as possible, is the job in hand. Presuming it is worth recovering then further considerations are necessary.

(2) *Assessing significance*

A major problem exists and one which justifies prime consideration. In order to concentrate fully on the problem, temporary delegation of duties connected with other enterprises should take place, if, and where, possible. Appointments may need to be cancelled and if this can be done by office staff or by a member of the family it will ease the load at this important time.

(3) *Considering alternatives*

This is where clear, but wide-range, thinking is required. The weather conditions which have caused the problem are most abnormal so that possible solutions may also be somewhat unusual. The thought often goes through the farmers mind, 'what will the neighbours think?', but if the crop is safely harvested surely that is the major objective. What then are some of the alternatives:

(a) Attract back to the field the married women who had to abandon picking due to the unsuitable conditions for young children. Hiring of the village hall with helpers to care for the children may be a possibility.
(b) With these useful facilities available, it would then be possible to advertise over a wider area in order to attract people who would not normally consider such work because of the tie of

young children. Hiring a coach or mini-bus to transport pickers from the nearest urban area could also be considered.
(c) Concentrate on weekend work when more local people are available, perhaps operating shifts so as to make full use of lifting machinery.
(d) Mechanical harvesting even if more damage is obtained. All local machinery will no doubt be in use so that contractors at a considerable distance may have to be approached despite the high cost of transporting their staff and machines.

(4) *Collecting information*

The telephone will be of most use in checking which of the above alternatives are possible and at what cost. Many pickers will not be on the phone so this will involve calling at their homes or putting advertisements in local village shops.

(5) *Evaluation*

Knowing the value of the crop in the ground will help to put a figure on the sum which can be justifiably spent in the recovery exercise. Although costs of the alternative solutions are relevant, the major issue is the one of timeliness and selecting a solution most likely to achieve the objective even if the weather conditions deteriorate further. Dependence upon mechanical harvesting would, therefore, be rated lower than trying to obtain extra hand pickers.

(6) *Choice*

After full evaluation, there may be few alternatives to choose from or the answer may well be in a combination of several solutions.

(7) *Implementation*

As with the strategic decision, this is a key area and will require continuous management input until all the crop is lifted. Organisation in the field as well as the transport and the children's 'playgroup' will need care and attention to detail.

(8) (9) Checking results and Responsibility

Evaluating progress on a daily basis will enable plans to be modified as the need arises. Considerable satisfaction will be obtained by all involved if a good decision is made and perhaps in future years pickers will be queuing at the field gate.

SOME QUESTIONS RELATING TO THIS CHAPTER

(1) To do nothing is to do something. Do you agree?
(2) How important a part of management is decision making?
(3) What part does judgement play in the decision making process?
(4) What is the difference between strategic and tactical decisions?
(5) What part do records of past performance play in decision making?
(6) Which has been the most important decision you have made in the last farming year?

A GUIDE TO SELECTED FURTHER READING

Drucker, P. F. 1968. *The Practice of Management.* London: Heinemann; London: Pan Books.
Read Chapter 28; as always Drucker gets first things first.

Hardaker, J. B. 1969. *Decision Trees: A Systematic Approach to Decision Making Under Uncertainty.* Farm Management Notes, no. 39, 9–18. Dept of Agricultural Economics, University of Nottingham.
A numerical but understandable and helpful guide to the decision maker who, even if he makes, 'sweeping simplifications' and constructs, 'a crude decision tree' will have, 'a better understanding of the choices he faces and of the risks he must bear'.

Norman, L. and R. B. Coote 1971. *The Farm Business.* London: Longman.
Chapters 2 and 5.

Barnard, C. S. and J. S. Nix 1973. *Farm Planning and Control.* Cambridge: Cambridge University Press.
Chapters 3 and 14.
The two books listed immediately above both set out some of the relevant arithmetic in the chapters indicated.

6
Control

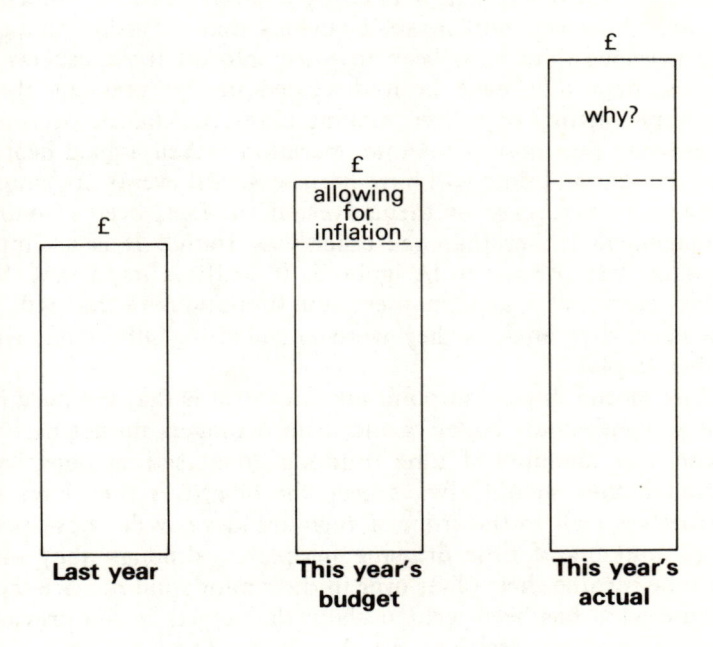

[Bar chart: "Last year" £; "This year's budget" £ with "allowing for inflation" marked; "This year's actual" £ with "why?" marked above a dashed line]

It is difficult not to claim for any chapter in this book that it may be the most important one. That is simply because each of the topics chosen *is* important in the context of the overall management task and the need for managers to be effective. If that is true of all the other topics in this book, it is certainly true of *control*. We have stated before that we are reluctant to think in terms of one topic being more important than any other, but if pressed, the need for effective control would come high on our list of priorities. Let us explain why.

THE IMPORTANCE OF CONTROL

We would single out three reasons for attaching so much importance to this topic. First, because it is concerned with actually *doing* what is intended; secondly, because it is a continuous requirement and thirdly, because without some form of control system, inadequate performance can easily be masked in any multi-enterprise business.

The first of these three reasons hardly needs elaboration, but like many obvious things, may easily be overlooked. A moment's thought, however, will make it obvious that if careful thought and precious time have been invested into all those aspects of management that have been discussed in the previous three chapters – setting objectives, making plans, and taking decisions in order to put those plans into operation – then a good deal of that thought and time will have been wasted if events are simply allowed to take care of themselves; if, in fact, events control management rather than the other way round. It is a simple message, but one not to be ignored. It really is important that events work out – and the inevitable limitations to that will be discussed later on – as they were intended to. Otherwise, why bother to plan?

The second important point about control is that the need for it is so continuous. Farmers and farm managers do not need to spend vast amounts of time thinking about setting objectives, although they should always keep the objectives they have set themselves well to the front of their minds; nor do they spend large amounts of time drawing up plans, although they may often be turning their plans over in their mind; and nor are they, despite what has been written about the subject in the previous chapter, making decisions all day long. They are, however, concerned *all* the time with operations being done properly, with timeliness, with care, and with the correct applications of technical know-how. If, as it is often claimed, many farm managers are – because of their backgrounds, training and experience – more at home out on the farm than they are in their offices, then control should not be an alien function to them. It is, in fact, what much of practical farming is about; making sure that, in a physical sense, the right things are done in the right way, by the right people, and, specially important, at the right time. It is the most continual part of the manager's job.

Third, and lastly, we regard an effective control system as very important if there is any danger at all of poor technical or economic performance being masked and left undetected. In farming this can very easily happen. We are not being critical if we observe that the number of farmers who farm without a detailed budget are in a substantial majority, even in the late nineteen seventies, twenty years and more since farm business management took root as a formal discipline. This, in turn, means that profit targets are, more often than not, unrelated to carefully thought out statements of what is likely to happen and what is reasonable. More usually they are derived from a more or less enlightened expectation of what the overall financial outcome might be, based on what has happened in the past, mentally adjusted for the effect of changing prices and costs. Sometimes it will be close to the mark and sometimes not. Whether the expectation is approximately reached or not, the approach offers no useful guide, as to what, in detail, ought to have happened in each sector of the farm or in each of the main cost centres. The ease with which one miscalculation can compensate for another can be frightening. Indeed, the situation in which an overall profit target is achieved – with no really detailed calculation as to how it should have been or was achieved – may be more dangerous in terms of undetected and therefore uncorrected defects, than when the target is not met. In the latter case, at least there will be no delusion and investigation is likely to be prompted. It is still the case, however, that despite moves towards simple and more specialised farming systems, most farms are comprised of a number of different enterprises, and several of the more important farm costs (e.g. labour and machinery) are shared between those enterprises. Final profits, therefore, usually stem from a good deal of interlocking of activities with the obvious possibility of the efficient compensating for the inefficient. It is a dangerous situation which is especially common in agriculture and requires careful monitoring. It is one of the main reasons why we regard control as being so important.

THE ESSENCE OF CONTROL

Before going on to discuss the application of control systems to farming, it is important that we should be quite clear about what, in essence, is involved. It is not a complicated concept although some confusion might arise because of the two levels at which the subject exists. There is, at the practical work-a-day level, the physical performance of tasks. It needs control and so will the supervision of the staff involved. This aspect of control is concerned with getting things done. But there is also the question of the end result, both in physical and in financial terms, and measurement against a target. In other industries this approach is known as budgetary control, and it is gradually getting wider acceptance in farming. It tends to be an office job, not an open air one.

Although these two aspects of control are widely separated in terms of when they occur and how often they occur, we prefer not to make too wide a distinction between them. They are both part of the same basic need to try to control events and the one – the physical performance, is incorporated in the other – the financial appraisal. Both parts of the job entail, in essence, the following steps: having an objective in mind; knowing how you intend to set about achieving it; knowing what you have achieved; relating achievement to the intention; understanding the magnitude and reasons for divergence; taking corrective action wherever possible and as soon as possible; renewing and, if necessary, adjusting targets for the next production cycle.

THE RELEVANCE OF THE TARGET

It is important to be clear about the nature of a target. Some farmers and managers with whom we have discussed this matter have not been clear about this at all. They are often confused by the term 'target', with its implication of something to aim at and which should, therefore, be slightly beyond reach. In our view, in the context of budgetary control, physical targets and financial budgets should be realistic, based on known levels of performance and related to likely financial prices and costs. Uncertainty and inflation simply increase the difficulty of the exercise, but they don't remove the need for it. The importance, also, of adequate consultation with staff, as in any consideration of future objectives and plans, should be obvious. Specialist staff may well have insights, often denied to overall managers, into what is possible within their enterprise and what is not. Their contribution should be welcomed and used.

Budgets of a different kind – break even budgets or budgets reflecting what might be achieved given higher levels of performance – will have their uses in other contexts. So far as control is concerned, however, budgets should depict simply the best estimate of what is really expected to happen. This does not mean that they are blueprints to be slavishly followed. Opportunities to improve on the budget should obviously not be rejected. They will, anyhow, help to compensate for the things that, inevitably, have disappointed. As we have already acknowledged few plans work out exactly as planned.

During a farming year, it will sometimes become apparent that initial expectations are either not going to be achieved or that they are going to be exceeded. In this sense the target becomes a moving one. It is then possible and, simply in terms of *having the best possible knowledge* of what the overall outcome is likely to be, it is sensible to adjust the budget accordingly. In control terms, however, there is a danger here. If budgets continue to be altered, throughout the year, for known changes in physical and financial events, the net result will be that the revised budget is always achieved. There will be no deviation from the plan and, apparently, no need for correction. Our advice in this situation would be to have two budgets; one to be adjusted and one not to be, and it is against the latter one, that the most meaningful comparisons can be made between actual and budgeted performance. It is in the light of that kind of comparison that corrective action can be instigated or future plans and budgets adjusted. The adjustable budget, on the other hand, will have been valuable in indicating, at the earliest possible moment, what the eventual outcome of a year's trading is likely to be.

APPLICATIONS TO FARMING

Having now considered the importance of control, what in essence it entails, and the nature of budgetary targets, we wish to mention some of the more practical aspects of applying such thinking to farming operations. There may be some overlap here with some of the general thoughts that have already been discussed, but we, nevertheless, wish to stress the following four points:

First, any attempt to apply control in a farm business – whether at the practical operational level or in the office as a budgetary exercise – will tend to be a dominantly physical exercise. *Exercising control* implies *taking action*, and to the extent that farmers tend to be 'price takers' rather than 'price makers', their action, at least in the short period, will centre essentially around the physical performance that they are trying to achieve. Close collaboration and discussion with staff will be an important ingredient in this. The endeavour will be to *grow* crops, to *feed* livestock and to *produce* livestock products.

Secondly, in order to allow the contribution from each enterprise to be properly unravelled, it is essential that budgetary targets are expressed in the appropriate detail and that achieved results are measured in a similar way, i.e. x cows, producing y units of milk at z units of cash each. By comparing the planned and actual amounts of production from each enterprise and the use of each item of costs in this way, it will be possible to assess how much, if any, difference between the two is attributable to: (a) the number of units involved (in this case, cows), (b) the yield per unit (i.e. milk per cow) and, (c) the price received for each unit of milk. Similar breakdowns will be possible on the cost side of the farm economy. The full arithmetic of this kind of analysis is not difficult and has been described by us elsewhere (see Giles, Further Reading). It has the merit of identifying very clearly where discrepancies lie, and of quantifying them. It helps managers to identify these discrepancies which (in the light of any underlying technical or economic reasons for them) could be most easily rectified, as well as identifying which of them are the most significant in terms of lost net revenue.

Although both the physical and the financial elements of budgets prepared for this purpose relate to the future, reliable records of past physical performance, preferably relating to several years rather than one, are, in our view, likely to be the best available guide to what will happen. They are not the useless historical data that some would have us believe.

Thirdly, the time periods to which targets relate will be determined, usually, by the kind of enterprise in question, but also, perhaps, by the inclinations in these matters of the individual concerned. It has always been our contention that a determination to apply control techniques, in some form or another, acceptable to the person undertaking the task, is far more important than the particular method used. We are not purists in these matters. Clearly, however, it is more important to have a monthly target for an enterprise like dairying, where the input : output situation will be changing from month to month, than it is for, say, cereal farming. In that case, a single annual target can suffice.

In general, our view on this question is that monthly or quarterly targets may be desirable for some enterprises and some inputs, and that these might be used with advantage to supplement annual targets for the whole farm economy. We are aware that quarterly and sometimes monthly projected cash flows for the whole farm are increasingly used in this respect and would applaud the practice where it seems helpful and palatable. This approach can, however, involve considerable work and effort in trying to reconcile apparent discrepancies between planned and actual results in particular time periods which have been caused simply through accidents in the timing of payments and receipts or in assumptions, before the event, about when those transactions might take place. Contrary, it seems, to a growing body of opinion, there are many farm situations in which we would not press the need for this particular approach.

The fourth point is closely related to the last in that, although all farming operations lend themselves to a periodic (usually annual) analysis of the kind under discussion, some enterprises and some inputs, lend themselves to *short period* control checks. This is the answer that must be given to those who are critical of annually-applied budgetary control methods on the grounds that errors should be detected and corrected while they are happening, and not at the end of some artificial (in the farming sense) accounting period. As a general proposition it would be difficult to disagree with that view, but the plain fact is that there are numerous aspects of farming, including much arable farming and some livestock rearing, as well as in the use of some resources (especially the more fixed ones), where little or no corrective action can be applied except when strategic planning and decision making is under way for the next production cycle.

By contrast, it is perfectly true that there are those enterprises such as dairying, pigs and poultry (commonly referred to as 'the factory enterprises') and those inputs which are in steady continuous use (e.g. concentrated feedingstuffs, labour, fuel and repairs) which do lend themselves to, and do require, short period control checks. In the livestock enterprises mentioned above, food is being dispensed daily, by staff, in order that it may be converted into livestock produce: milk, young pigs or pigmeat and eggs. Efficient food conversion, in these circumstances, is vital and is to a considerable extent in the hands (i.e. the control) of those carrying out the operation. Careful records are required of the amount of food being used in any time period, its cost, and for the amount and value of the produce being generated by this process. We believe that it is important, in order to simplify the control process, to concentrate the recording process of those four items – the ones that determine the vital input : output ratio – and to disregard most other measurements. An increasingly large number of enterprise costing or control schemes are available to farmers sponsored by various organisations in the 'ancillary' sector and we are concerned that some of these are inclined to over-complicate the issues involved; perhaps because they are designed to provide information for the sponsors as well as for the farmer himself; perhaps, also, because of the existence of computers. There is need for discrimination in these areas.

So far as inputs are concerned, we would differentiate in our minds between those which flow continually, like a stream, and those which are controlled like water from a tap. Labour, fuel and feedingstuffs are all of the 'stream' type of expenditure and some form of regular check (possibly like the histogram at the beginning of this chapter) seems desirable, just in case the stream turns into a flood. The payment, on the other hand, of rent, and the purchase of items like seeds, fertilisers and sprays are more akin to the 'tap' situation. The tap is briefly turned on and then turned off and when it is off no further control is required. It is, therefore, within the 'factory' enterprises and in the areas of 'stream' expenditure that most scope exists for the application of short period control checks. They should be used, we suggest, as a supplement to a more comprehensive annual check on everything. It is in these areas where the frequent checks are required and where targets may need to be set from month to month simply because the physical events (especially in the dairy and poultry enterprises) will vary from month to month.

Finally, in considering the application of control methods to farming it must, of course, be admitted that there will be many factors influencing both farming operations themselves and the financial outcome of those operations which will be quite outside the control of any manager. The list of those influences hardly needs reproducing. It will make familiar reading to those in the industry. The weather, disease, world market forces, government and international agricultural and economic policies; all of these and more will, from time to time, exert their unexpected influences, but not always in a way which is detrimental to all farmers, and certainly not exclusively towards farmers. Budgetary control is not really about these influences. It is about identifying what has not gone according to plan, measuring the extent of that occurrence, discovering why it happened, identifying the extent to which management can or cannot bring about a correction, and then, where it can, bringing it about. The fact that some of the reasons for failure to achieve a desired result are outside the control of management is neither here nor there. It is certainly not an argument to be used against the application of control methods in farming. On the contrary, we would argue that the more influences at work that are outside the control of management, the more important it becomes to identify items that can be controlled and for careful control then to be exercised. The existence of influences outside the control of management could, therefore, call for a greater application of budgetary control rather than less.

CONTROL AT THE HEART OF MATTERS

We have tried to demonstrate in this chapter the importance of control and some particular features of its applications in a farming business. Perhaps more than any other topic in this book it comes close to the heart of farming itself. But it also comes close to the heart of effective management and in this sense draws closely together the two disciplines with which this book is concerned; farming and management. We felt it to be important, therefore, that the chapter should close with a few general comments to emphasise the significance of control in this cohesive role. Several points, in particular, need to be made.

First, budgetary control is not just about arithmetic. The arithmetic that is involved can and should be simple. It should enlighten, not confuse. Its main purpose is to direct managers to where corrective action is required. Without that corrective action, no control will have been exercised. With it, effective farming practice and effective management through control will have been combined in an attempt to produce required results. Where this is brought about with the co-operation and contribution of employees, budgetary control will have had a particularly important bonding effect.

Secondly, budgetary control offers the most relevant and pertinent way in which farmer-managers can assess the overall financial results from their businesses in any particular year. It enables them to judge their results against a tailor-made statement of what *they* consider to be possible, on *their* farm, under *their* management, during the precise twelve months in question. It is, therefore, a substantially sharper tool than comparative analysis which involves the comparison of results on one farm with 'standards' of performance based on the average or above average results for a group of farms. That is not to suggest that comparative analysis is not useful. Its critics, we believe, have always expected too much of it. In a competitive industry it is totally reasonable for individuals to wish to know how they compare with groups of other individuals in roughly similar situations, especially with those individuals at the top end of the profitability scale. Most farmers fully appreciate that no two situations are the same and that precise deductions from individual figures, without regard to the whole picture, would be dangerous. In this limited sense, the 'league table' spirit is understandable and it is an area of business management in which agriculture, over the years, has often led the field. We recognise its use, but also its limitations and it is because of these limitations that we would urge farmers towards a budgetary assessment of their results, in addition to, if not as a complete substitute for, comparative analysis. That means, quite simply, that a complete and detailed budget for each ensuing year should be an automatic part of every farmer's managerial equipment. We know, of course, that is still very far from being the case, even in the most developed countries.

Thirdly – and this brings us back to the importance of farming techniques and husbandry – we believe it is right to suggest to farmers that, in their quest for increased profit, there is often more scope for achieving this by improving the level of performance of what is currently being done than by searching for radically different systems of farming. Our observation tells us that the majority of farm systems are reasonably well suited to the resources – including the managers – that are available. If that were not the case it would imply that farmers are bad judges of what is right for them and their farms and we do not believe that to be the case. Earlier reference, however, to the very wide performance gap which is known to exist in the industry would tend to confirm our contention about the scope for tightening up on technical performance and economic organisation *within existing* enterprises; and that is precisely what budgetary control and supervisory control are concerned with. For the record, we should add that we are not suggesting that nobody should try to do anything new. Sometimes, of course, it will be necessary. But we are saying, think carefully before you do so and, first, look critically at what you already have and at the possibility for improving it.

Finally, in this chapter, we simply wish to draw attention to the common thought that underlies budgetary control – the attempt to do what you intend to do as well as you can – and the concept of key results areas discussed in our chapter on objectives. Again, from our observation, we have come to the view that on many farms there are only a few (sometimes only one) important aspects of management, e.g. yields on the arable farm; margin over concentrates per forage acre on the dairy farm; food costs per £100 output on the pig farm, which *really* matter, and to which, therefore, unlimited care and effort should be applied. That thought underlies management by objectives and it also underlies the concept and techniques of control. It is a theme to which we shall return in our penultimate chapter on priorities.

SOME QUESTIONS RELATING TO THIS CHAPTER

(1) Do you agree that control is primarily a physical matter?
(2) Which of your enterprises lend themselves to short period control and which do not?
(3) How valuable do you think monthly and/or quarterly projected cash flows can be in exercising control?
(4) Control is mainly an office job. Do you agree?
(5) What role do you think employees can play in establishing and applying control systems?
(6) Control is the most continual of all management tasks. Do you agree?
(7) The existence of factors outside the manager's control calls for more endeavour to control, not less. Do you agree?

A GUIDE TO SELECTED FURTHER READING

Giles, A. K. 1964. *Budgetary Control as an aid to Farm Management.* Miscellaneous Study no. 33. Dept of Agricultural Economics and Management, University of Reading.
Describes the arithmetic of budgetary control.

Sizer, J. 1969. *An Insight into Management Accounting.* West Drayton, Middlesex: Penguin Books.
Chapter 7 (Budgetary control) is a helpful chapter in a generally helpful book.

Budgetary Control in Farm Management, 1975. Bulletin no. 10. North of Scotland College of Agriculture.
Provides some useful examples.

Part III
WHAT HAS TO BE MANAGED

7
Production

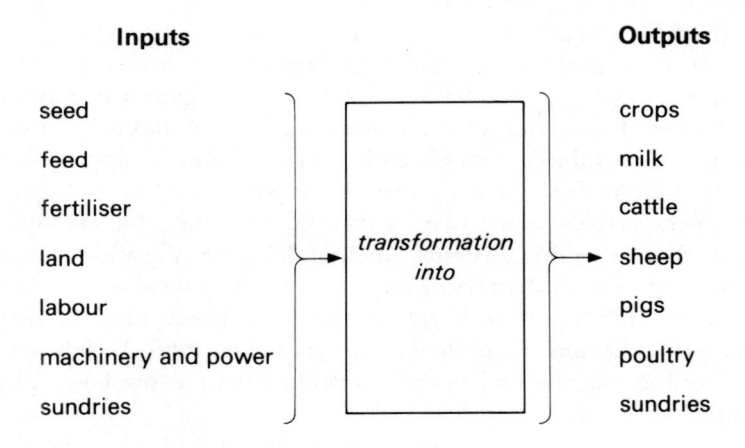

Inputs		Outputs
seed		crops
feed		milk
fertiliser		cattle
land	transformation into	sheep
labour		pigs
machinery and power		poultry
sundries		sundries

THE CONCEPT OF PRODUCTION

The concept of production is an elusive one. In some respects it is straightforward enough; it is after all, what farming is really all about – the creation of commodities that, either directly or indirectly, will be turned into food or drink for human consumption. The moment, however, one begins to reflect on precisely what is involved – *on how production is actually brought about* – then the subject begins to become more complex and more elusive.

There are, of course, reasons for this complexity. Production is the co-ordinating process which brings together capital and labour in its various forms – raw materials, processed goods and equipment of all kinds, plant, technology, the work force and management – in order to *create* the *commodity* or, perhaps increasingly in agriculture, the *service* that is required. It is, however, difficult for us to visualise production in the way that we can identify and visualise in our mind's eye factors of production such as land or a piece of machinery, or even some of the managerial functions that have been discussed in earlier chapters. In farming, we cannot always *see* production while it is happening and sometimes we cannot even *measure* it, at least until the end of a production cycle.

In these circumstances we may be tempted to turn to the literature of farming and farm management in order to find a proper perspective on the subject, but here again we may be frustrated. Production so often means different things to different people. The subject is so all embracing and can be approached from so many different specialised standpoints, that overall views and perspectives tend to be easily lost. We may, for example, read about farming systems, about labour organisation, about technology and husbandry or about the application of operational research techniques to farming. Each of these subjects may purport to be about production and yet we may still be left with the feeling that the real essence of production has not been fully explained to us.

In this situation it may be tempting to conclude that there is no such thing as a separate and identifiable production process; that it is merely the result of the co-ordination of various other processes which require specialised resources and skills. But that view, of course, would be to deny the all important contribution from management in co-ordinating inputs in a way that transforms them into outputs. Far from denying the existence of production as a process, therefore, we are of the view that it is one of the central responsibilities – if not *the* central responsibility – of management. As suggested earlier, it is at the very heart of farming itself and it is not surprising that continuing financial success in a farming business will often, in the last resort, depend upon the ability of the manager to organise an effective *production system*.

THE ESSENCE OF PRODUCTION

Having recognised the complex and elusive nature of production, and having placed it at the heart of the business and managerial function, it is now necessary to state in more detail what we believe it entails. Any such statement will clearly be open to debate and individual interpretation, but for all practical purposes, we see three essential parts to production:

(a) Building a production plan, having due regard to market opportunities, available fixed resources, and the facility for adjustment.
(b) Acquiring the necessary resources and employing them in the appropriate combination.
(c) Operating the plan, with due regard to required levels of performance and appropriate supervision.

Each of these three topics will be discussed more fully in the remainder of this chapter but before proceeding to that we wish to digress, briefly, in order to discuss one or two economic concepts which we believe to be important and relevant.

First, we wish to mention the concept of *effective demand*. It was hinted at in our definition of management in Chapter 2 when we referred to the production of a commodity or service which is both wanted and can be offered at a price that will be paid. This concept underlies much of what follows in this chapter. In economic terms demand always means effective demand. It implies that the desire to buy something on the part of an individual or a group of individuals is backed by an ability and willingness to buy at a given price.

Hardly surprisingly this concept has vital implications for the producer. Under normal competitive conditions, where a market price is determined *for* rather than *by* him, he will need to produce at a level of economic efficiency which, at the reigning prices of the commodities he is selling, will yield an acceptable profit. If that is not the case, then sooner or later he will be out of business. At any given set of prices and costs he will, therefore, be concerned with *economic efficiency rather than with technical efficiency that ignores effective demand*. As a matter of fact we are not quite sure how to define the term 'technical efficiency'. If, however, it implies some notion of a technically perfect animal or crop, produced without blemish and with the highest quality materials and care, but for which there is no effective demand, then it is not a very helpful concept to the farmer who wishes to remain in business. This is not, of course, to deny the merits of doing things well within the limits of existing prices and costs. We have already noted, in an earlier chapter, that it is the *final* litres of milk and tonnes of grain which add to profit. It often costs as much to do things badly as to do them well, so that doing things well in this productive sense is usually in harmony with economic efficiency; and even if farmers and farm managers are not always interested in literally maximising profits, at the end of the day they simply cannot ignore the need for economic efficiency. On the contrary they will often twist and turn in reaching their decisions about *what* to produce, *what methods* to use, and *how much* to produce in an endeavour to generate profits which are acceptable to them in their particular circumstances.

Economists embrace these three questions – what to produce, by what methods to produce and how much to produce – in their so-called 'theory of the firm'. It describes those conditions which have to exist if profits are to be maximised. It is not necessary for practising farmers to have a detailed knowledge of this theory, but to the extent that it underlies some of the principles and tools that are used in elementary farm planning, a brief word about it is appropriate.

The question of *what to produce* is referred to (in economists' jargon) as a product – product type of question. It relates to the combination of one enterprise with another, or with others. Equilibrium will be reached (i.e. the point where there is no further incentive to change the combination) when, at any given set of prices and costs, equal returns are being received from the last unit of capital employed in each enterprise. Equi-marginal returns are then said to exist. If greater returns accrued from the marginal use of capital in one enterprise, as opposed to another, then a further direction of capital to that enterprise would be indicated.

The question of *what methods to employ* within an enterprise (i.e. how much machinery, how much labour, and so on) is known as a factor – factor question. It has that name because it is concerned with the combination of factors of production, rather than with the combination of enterprises, and, again, equilibrium will be reached – there being no further incentive to change –

when the last unit of capital spent on one factor of production yields the same return as the last unit spent on any other. If this were not the case a redirection of capital in favour of one factor at the expense of another would be called for – concentrated food instead of fertiliser on grass, for example.

Thirdly, the question of *how much to produce*, is known as a factor – product question, in which equilibrium is reached when the last unit of capital spent in any direction (the marginal cost) equals the additional receipts generated (the marginal revenue). To stop short of this point (i.e. when marginal costs are still below the marginal revenue) would be to ignore some remaining opportunities of gain, however small. To go beyond it (where costs become greater than receipts) would be to begin to incur losses.

Overall, equilibrium will only have been reached when there is no incentive to change in any of the three directions that we have discussed, i.e. in the combination of enterprises, in the methods of production and in the overall scale of production.

BUILDING A PRODUCTION PLAN

That was, perhaps, a rather long excursion into economic thinking, stemming from the mention of effective demand, technical efficiency and economic efficiency. We can now revert to the more familiar farming scene. It will, no doubt, have been clear to the reader that very few farmers need to think precisely in the ways that have just been outlined. All kinds of practical considerations prohibit this. There is, for instance, the simple fact that most of them do not necessarily aim to maximise profits; the fact that very often, because of the complications of costs that are shared between enterprises, farmers will not know, in detail, the marginal costs associated with each of their enterprises; because extra inputs of lumpy resources like labour and machinery, for example, cannot be employed in small incremental units; and because there are such personal feelings as caution, not wanting to farm to the brink, and having regard for the long term consequences of farming decisions as well as the short term ones. Nevertheless farmers will be familiar with the questions that were posed in the preceding paragraphs. They *will* consider carefully the allocation of land, labour and capital between the different enterprises on their farms; they *will* explore ways and means (taking due notice of research and development work) of producing in a 'least cost' way; and they *will* have to decide how intensive they should become – recognising, for instance, when *increasing returns* seem likely to give way to *diminishing returns.*

Notwithstanding these various constraints that inhibit them from applying economic theory in practice, farmers and their advisers will and do find it useful to pick out the pieces of theory that help. A good example of this is the general recognition now given by the farming community to the distinction between fixed and variable cost – a distinction which is at the heart of the *gross margin* concept, so commonly used in farm planning. With these background thoughts in mind, however, we can now turn more directly to the question of farm planning and consider, in turn, three generally recognised approaches to building a production plan. They vary in their degree of sophistication and are as follows:

First, there are methods based on *simple subjective decisions* made by farmers in the face of the resources at their disposal, on what has been happening previously, and on their personal experience and inclinations. This is not a sophisticated approach but it should not be criticised for that. It may be especially appropriate where there is little or no choice of activity and where the farmer's own judgement is proven. It is also important to remember that when an individual is doing what he wants to do he is likely to produce the best results anyhow. A system of farming embarked upon in this way can be evaluated by orthodox budgeting in which the physical elements of the plan (i.e. the number of livestock, acres of crops, and resources needed) will be priced in order to arrive at the predicted profit. There are many, many farms where the production plans have originated and evolved, with the passing of time, in this way. Many such farms are known to us personally and we would, in no way, denigrate the approach. It relies on experience, judgement, and intuition – valuable attributes in any manager.

Secondly, there are those methods which rely on a more *systematic* and *objective assessment.* All of these methods have in common that they employ the gross margin concept in one form or another. At the most elementary level, gross margins are calculated and then enterprises are selected in descending order of gross margin per unit. We will discuss the gross margin a little further on in this chapter. For the moment it is sufficient to say that it measures the difference between the output from the enterprise and the variable costs incurred in achieving that output and, hence, the contribution that each unit of that enterprise can make towards covering the fixed costs of the farm and providing a final profit. The gross margin is not the profit itself. Used in this elementary way the gross margin approach to planning may provide only a slight advance on the subjective method just discussed. At the other end of the gross margin scale, however, it may be used, still in a hand-operated way, to select a production system which takes full account of the available resources, the possible enterprises and the constraints operating on both. Such methods – and there are numerous variations on the theme – are known collectively, as 'programme planning'. We will return to them in a moment.

The third basic approach to building a farm plan is where, because of the complexity of the available choices between enterprises and the range of resource constraints, recourse is made to a computer. Several *computerised planning methods* are in existence, the most well known of them being linear programming. There is plenty of evidence that such techniques are a helpful aid to advisers and consultants in arriving at modal farm plans that can be adapted to individual circumstances. There is, however, despite a lot of development work by various advisory agencies, little evidence to suggest that these kinds of approach are being widely used on individual farms, and, personally, we do not envisage the situation changing substantially in the near future. Such techniques usually require an experienced adviser, backed by computer resources and personnel that may or may not have to be paid for by the client, and, despite the speed with which profit-maximising solutions can be generated once problems have been properly formulated, the overall time involved will usually have to concede something to more 'back of the envelope' methods – just as *those* methods will have to concede something to computer methods in their objectivity, accuracy and the depth in which they demand that production possibilities and problems are explored.

Our considered reflection on these three basically different approaches to farm planning is that while traditional budgeting may still suffice in many cases, the time is arriving when, certainly in the more complex farming situations, something more systematic and objective will often be desired. But at the same time, we would hold that there is a very large number of farms where the basic planning problem is insufficiently complicated to warrant computerised methods, which do, of course, have the disadvantage that they are unlikely to be able to be applied by the farmer or manager himself.

This reasoning leads us to the conclusion that some variant of the second approach – sometimes known as 'ordered budgeting' – is probably the most appropriate planning tool on many farms that we know. It does not seem to matter too much which particular variant of this approach is used. What is important is the systematic and the objective nature of the approach. Our plea, therefore, is for the building of farm production plans involving something like the following combination of steps:

(a) A detailed consideration of the resources that are available – land, labour and capital – with special recognition of which is most scarce.
(b) A review of the available marketing opportunities and requirements – with a special regard for 'effective demand'.
(c) A consideration, in the light of (a) and (b) and of personal preferences, of all of the enterprises that could comprise the production programme – not necessarily confined to existing ones.
(d) The calculation of the 'normalised' gross margins (i.e. taking account of known performance over a number of years and anticipated future costs and prices) for each of the enterprises, using published 'standard' data, appropriately adapted, for new enterprises. The gross margins should be expressed in terms of the unit of the scarcest resource, and more often than not, in this country, it will be land.
(e) A consideration of the various physical limits that must be set to the scale of each enterprise, depending upon the existence of such factors as buildings, rotational considerations, seasonal deadlines, quotas and the farmer's own personal preferences.
(f) The selection of each enterprise, in descending order of gross margin per unit, to its predetermined limit, continuing until the scarcest resource is exhausted.
(g) A check that no other scarce resource has been exhausted. If it has (e.g. labour or capital) explore the possibilities of

Building a production plan

expanding the supply of that resource, or substituting into the plan, some (or more) of any enterprise that has yet to reach its limit and which will reduce the demands on the resource in question to acceptable levels.
(h) The possible introduction of other enterprises making no demands on the scarcest resource, e.g. intensive livestock.
(i) The calculation of total gross margin for the final selection of enterprises.
(j) The subtraction of fixed costs from total gross margin to determine the profit.

In advocating this systematic approach to building the farm plan we are aware that there are those who would disagree with us and who would contend that it lacks both the ease of the more subjective approach and the precision of the more objective ones; that the arithmetic can, in fact, become fairly complicated and that, in short, the method falls between two stools. We accept that there is some force in these arguments, but, just as forcibly, we would argue that unless the process is made complicated by the user, the arithmetic can be kept fairly simple; that the result will be based upon more rigorous and methodical thinking than the *ad hoc* approach of subjective budgeting; and that – an important point in our minds – the method (unlike computerised ones) can be applied, personally, by any of the farmers and farm managers to whom this book is addressed.

It is, of course, common to *all* methods of farm planning that any chosen programme relates to a given set of fixed resources. If those resources are then altered, the situation calls for a re-selection of the enterprises that would be feasible and sensible in those changed circumstances.

This chapter is already in some danger of becoming over-long, which perhaps reflects the central importance that we attach to its subject matter. We have still to consider the questions of *acquiring resources* and *operating the plan*. Before doing so, however, there are two other topics that must be mentioned: adjusting plans, and gross margins.

Adjusting the plan

Important though devising the plan in the first place may be, it is not something that has to be done too often; once a year at the most and to the extent that circumstances may not call for a radical alteration, perhaps less often than that. It will, however, be essential to keep a constant and critical eye on the need to adjust the plan slightly from time to time, if only to meet the consequences of constantly changing prices and costs.

A systematic approach to this rather nagging aspect of farm planning can be as helpful as it is in devising an overall plan in the first place. In this context we have found it helpful to explore the opportunities for profit-improving adjustments within the framework of the following four different kinds of change:

(a) Improving gross margins within existing enterprises, whether as a result of physical input : output improvements, marketing improvements or in the purchase and use of variable costs. The possibilities here are endless. They are at the very heart of production.
(b) Altering the system of farming, by substitutions at the margin, in favour of enterprises yielding the higher gross margins. This could include the introduction of entirely new enterprises and, coupled with possible reductions in fixed costs, changes in the reverse direction. System changes of this kind will encourage a constant re-appraisal of just where realistic limits to enterprises really lie. Changes in economic circumstances have often been known to create changes in thinking about what is and what is not possible.
(c) Reducing fixed costs, with or without a change in the pattern of enterprises.
(d) Adding to the economic base of the business, by the introduction of fresh land, new enterprises not requiring land, or new non-farming activities.

We believe that every possible kind of change can be considered under one or other of these four headings and we would encourage periodic and systematic reviews of farm businesses in this way. The time will come when the opportunities to improve, under each heading, will begin to be exhausted and this fact should not be overlooked. Improving gross margins, for instance, will require improved management in one form or another and, even where this is possible, that possibility will diminish as each improvement is achieved, unless there are favourable changes in market prices. Diminishing returns are, sooner or later, a real barrier to the

Diagrammatically these four possible ways of adding to profit can be represented in the following model of a three-enterprise farm:

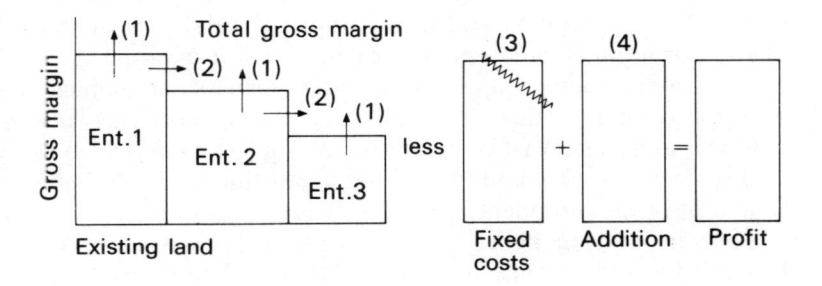

[Diagram: Stacked bars labeled Ent.1, Ent.2, Ent.3 on "Existing land" showing Gross margin with arrows (1) and (2) indicating Total gross margin, less (3) Fixed costs + (4) Addition = Profit]

endless intensification of farming methods. Sooner or later, also, husbandry or other practical considerations will call a halt to adjustments to farming systems. Reductions in fixed costs may sometimes be possible especially in the sphere of machinery or labour costs, but it is seldom the case that reductions of this kind can be repeated. Lumpy inputs, like labour and machinery, really are indivisible. Finally, an expansion of the economic base of the business will usually require new capital, possibly some new skills and maybe some degree of luck (as when extra land becomes available in a convenient site and at an acceptable price) and none of these things can be made to order.

Just in case the last paragraph has a pessimistic sound to it, let it be said that there are no farms that we know where the possibilities under all four of our headings have yet run out. Few farmers would claim that each enterprise on their farm was being operated at optimum efficiency, with no scope whatever for improvement and few, also, would feel there was no scope for adjustment in their system. Changing a system slightly can sometimes be the most painless kind of change to make. It does not call for better management, but simply for a different combination of activities. Trying to become better at something may be more difficult, and it is in that area, no doubt, that the advisory services have their particular part to play. At all events, we would urge that every possibility of improving the use of *existing* resources should be thoroughly explored before new activities, requiring *new* resources, are introduced.

The gross margin

Frequent reference has been made in this chapter to the gross margin. Its use has been embodied in the most favoured method of initial farm planning and in the approach to reviewing such plans. Consultants, advisers and teachers find it a valuable tool in this context. Increasingly, it seems, that farmers and managers also recognise its value. This has not always been the case, however, and some brief comment on the subject seems called for at this stage. Much could be written about this much maligned little unit of measurement, but a few words must suffice.

Contrary to some belief, it is not a particularly new concept. It first appeared, in embryo form, in Reading University, as far back as the early 1920s and, some years later, appeared again in the publication of farm income data in Northern Ireland. Its first major use as a management tool in England, however, was in the Eastern Counties in the early 1960s, when David Wallace, of Cambridge University, recognised its value in a farming locality where the *choice* of enterprises was of paramount importance. It does not, as we have already said, measure profit. It is an inappropriate measure, for instance, in price-fixing discussions when, understandably, farmers will wish *all* costs – not just the variable ones – to be taken into account. When, however, a farming system, and modifications to it are being considered, that is not necessarily the case. Fixed costs often do remain fixed in the face of minor modifications to a system and in those circumstances it is the effect of variations in output and variable costs which need to be explored. This does not mean that fixed costs will never *alter* in magnitude, even in the short term – inflation alone will see to that. But it does mean that various enterprise combinations may be possible – and that *small* alterations to a system will be possible – without necessarily altering the level of fixed costs. The fact that the so-called fixed costs (regular labour, machinery, rent and overheads) are likely to vary considerably in magnitude from farm to farm, and that the variable costs (materials and casual labour) often do not, is an irrelevance.

To the extent that the gross margin calculation measures, in one composite figure, the effect of the physical efficiency with which an individual converts certain variable inputs (with the help of other more fixed inputs) into a saleable product, it is a valuable indicator of efficiency within an enterprise on a particular farm. Other farms, however, may well use resources in different combinations (more regular labour for instance – a fixed cost; and less casual labour – a variable cost) so that inter-farm comparisons of gross margins can be dangerous. Equally dangerous is the assumption that when small changes occur on a particular farm, changes in profitability can *always* be measured simply by manipulating gross margins. The possibility of lumpy changes in the fixed costs must always be looked for. How and when they occur will depend on the situation on the farm in question. Two farms, making identical farming changes may well be 'jumping off' from different starting points and the effect of the change on the fixed costs may be quite different in the two circumstances. That is why the use of the partial budget, which looks at every item of cost and return that undergoes change, is often what is required. Gross margins can be part of that process. Sometimes they will suffice by themselves but sometimes they will not – depending upon the scale and type of change that is involved. It should never, therefore, be assumed that gross margins are totally adequate by themselves and no farmer or adviser who understands the data he is handling will be in danger of making that assumption.

We must leave gross margins at this point except to add that they now form an established and accepted part of farm management thinking. To the extent that, in Europe at least, there is also a growing tendency to present global financial results for different farming systems in the gross margin and fixed cost form, and that gross margins are now being used as a basis for measuring farm size and type, we may reasonably expect to find this measure in increased rather than reduced use in the years ahead. Anyone in the United Kingdom looking for examples of gross margins for different enterprises – with an indication of all the variables that they can embrace – can do no better than to refer to an up-to-date issue of the Farm Management Pocketbook, prepared periodically by John Nix at Wye College.

Finally, here, we would just like to add that if, alongside the use of gross margins, there is a renewed desire on the part of some farmers to have recourse to more fully costed enterprise budgets and statements of results, we have some sympathy with that desire and will comment on it in our chapter dealing with finance.

ACQUIRING AND EMPLOYING THE REQUIRED RESOURCES

Having developed an optimal plan in terms of utilising the major resources of land, labour, capital and management ability, then the operation of the plan involves the provision of a wide range of additional resources and here we are right back into practical farming. The required resources include everyday items such as fuel and spare parts, seed, feedingstuffs or replacement breeding stock as well as the services of specialists such as contractors or veterinarians. The manager needs to know where to obtain these resources, a subject that will be discussed in more detail in Chapter 12, but he has also to consider how much of the resource to buy, the price, quality, timeliness of delivery and the date when payment is due. In addition, it is necessary with many inputs to consider the transport, unloading arrangements and required storage facilities. In practice, it is seldom possible to have the best of all worlds and decisions have to be made, arriving at a compromise situation. Take, for instance, a cereal grower purchasing seed for autumn use. Early ordering and delivery widens the choice of variety and grade, it enables increased discounts to be obtained but it may well involve earlier payment. Reception of the consignment ahead of planting time ensures that the seed is on hand for timely drilling, but it involves storage, double-handling or the use of trailers or other vehicles which are not then available for other purposes. The chances of producing higher yields of a quality product are increased by using appropriate resources at the optimum time. The increased value of output will more than cover additional costs leaving an improved margin for the efficient 'obtainer of resources'. It is seen once again that the manager's task involves planning, making decisions and, especially, getting priorities right.

The time and effort required by management to obtain resources varies considerably from one type to another. Inputs such as electricity and water flow into the farm as required, with usage easily measured and therefore not difficult to record. Emergency breaks to supply can be aided by staff having a list of appropriate telephone numbers available as well as site plans which indicate supply routes and the location of switches or stop valves. Many other farm inputs such as fuel, feedingstuffs and fertilisers are ordered without difficulty according to recognised grades or specification. Specialised advice may be required before an order can be placed for chemical pesticides or animal medicines.

In order to receive delivery of a required input at the appropriate time, several factors have to be taken into account. First, the time lag between placement of the order and expected delivery. Secondly, the rate of use, which is often obtained from a recording scheme, and thirdly, the quantity in stock. Having this information readily to hand is an important area of efficient production management. It involves such factors as the neat and tidy stacking of stores, graduated marks on the walls of storage bins and dipsticks or sight glasses for use with liquid tanks. As well as enabling quick and accurate stock-taking to take place, such aids and procedures encourage accurate record keeping. A system for checking deliveries, filing delivery notes and issuing despatch documents is another important aspect of this subject. With the increasing tendency to handle commodities in bulk, there is the need to install weighing devices so as to be able to monitor, as required, the inputs and outputs of production.

The farm staff need to understand their role and authority in obtaining resources. Procedures for calling the vet, ordering fuel or obtaining spare parts need to be discussed, agreed and perhaps committed to paper. Managers may wish and be able to delegate the task of ordering routine inputs but they should at all times be kept 'in the picture'. In the larger businesses, routine reports may be prepared by section heads which cover this item or an arrangement whereby the manager signs official orders to confirm telephone orders from employees.

With the increasing trend towards mechanisation and automation of farms, coupled with the wide range of models in use, the supply of spare parts is becoming a most important part of production management. Reliance on mechanical feeding equipment or manure handling in livestock units involves the vital need for prompt repair of breakdowns, but equally in arable farming, delays to planting, spraying or harvesting operations by lack of spares can be a costly item. Cash flow considerations on the part of dealers and agents result in minimal stocks of spares being carried locally thus involving the need to contact manufacturers direct, arrange long distance transport or perhaps co-operate in the holding of spares with other local users of identical equipment. Instruction books and spare parts lists need to be readily available from files in the office or workshop with another copy left with the operator. A very efficient labelling and re-ordering system has been observed on one farm, where each sizeable part in the farm workshop store carries a label bearing the name of the supplier and the part number. When a member of staff uses a part, the label is removed, put into a tray, and then forms the basis of a shopping list. The label is tied to the new part on arrival which is then put back on the shelf. Such a system aids day-to-day management of a busy farm and at the same time demonstrates to staff that management is prepared to provide an efficient back-up service.

Adjustments to a production plan will at times also necessitate the need for additional inputs of the major resources such as land and buildings. The difficulty, for example, in providing adequate straw and labour for bedding in a beef unit may justify the installation of slatted floors to the fattening buildings. Such a modification, providing that adequate ventilation and trough space are available, would enable the stocking density in the pens to be almost doubled. Assuming that the working capital was available to purchase additional stock, then the limiting resource would probably be land to provide additional forage feeds. Modification to the cropping plan may be a possibility but another alternative would be to lease an acreage from a neighbouring holding in order to grow a crop of maize for silage. Expanding the area of land, if on a temporary basis, can also have advantages in spreading the cost of expensive machinery such as pea viners or a grass drier. A sheep farmer known to us, takes land from adjacent cereal growers for a two year ley break in order to expand the size of his flock. He provides seed, fertiliser and fences, removing his stock in time for early ploughing of the second year ley for wheat. Few problems arise, but considerable time was initially involved negotiating the mutually satisfactory arrangement, especially the method of calculating the charge. There are obvious attractions to farming additional land especially to the person who has, as a long term objective, the one of increasing the size of business. The location of additional fields as well as any specific difficulties such as access or the availability of water have a marked effect upon their contribution to the overall business. Travelling between blocks of land is not only expensive in machinery costs, but it occupies time and aggravates the situation that when problems do arise, managers tend to be in the wrong part of the farm.

Opportunities to improve the output potential of existing acres should not be overlooked before expanding the size of a farm. Improvements to drainage, lime status, sward quality of permanent pasture, field size and shape do have a marked effect upon economic efficiency.

The need to increase building capacity is common in many farming situations. Legislation in the UK has, for instance, created the need for specialised chemical stores and, for participation in the brucellosis eradication scheme with cattle, the requirement for isolation pens.

Technological developments enable additional capital to be justifiably invested, as with facilities to store produce resulting from higher yields or new varieties. In animal production, there is, for example, the justification for specialised flat-deck cages to accommodate piglets weaned at three weeks of age or storage facilities for the components of complete cattle diets. Considerable management input is essential in planning for farm buildings, not only in regard to the financial implications but also to their location, layout, appearance, maintenance and future expansion.

Chapter 10 is essentially about the management of staff, but it is appropriate to mention at this point, the many situations in which an additional, but temporary, input of labour is required. Many intensive fruit and vegetable enterprises operate with a small permanent staff but depend to a large extent upon obtaining sufficient casual workers to plant, prune, harvest and grade their crops. The processing of turkeys and capons for the Christmas trade is another example of an enterprise where in order to provide the market with a fresh, high quality product at the optimum time, an additional short term labour input may be required. The people doing such jobs often return to the same farm each year, and although the work may in some circumstances be rather unpleasant, because it is only for a short period the workers enjoy the change and make the most of the 'extra' money. Where skills are required, they are seldom lost from one year to another but such workers vary widely in the degree of supervision required. Involvement of regular full-time staff with the part-time team needs to be handled with care. Regulars should understand that they are the key workers, but casuals will not be keen to return on future occasions if they feel that they are not appreciated and if always given the dirty jobs.

The majority of farms need from time to time, to employ specialists who bring into the business skills which are not available in the regular staff, such as the veterinary surgeon or the seed crop inspector. The particular skills may even be available as with the shepherd and the job of shearing but due to pressure of other work, it may in some circumstances be preferable to employ the skilled help in order to get the job done more quickly and more efficiently. Contractors usually use their own equipment, which being in regular use and perhaps a more up-to-date model, operates at a higher rate than if farm equipment was used. Mechanical hedge trimming is such an example, in that the latest rotary flail models shred the trimmings so that no hand raking and burning is needed, as was the case with older machines.

The cost of employing a specialist does 'on the face' often appear to be high, especially when the skills and the machinery already exist in the business. A calculation to evaluate the effect of timeliness on the operations that would be delayed by not employing help, indicates the sum that can be justifiably spent on the additional input. The contractor who provides efficiently operated machinery is becoming a more important resource to a wide range of farming situations. With the cost of purchasing and maintaining specialised items of equipment continuing to increase, the contractor will find an expanding demand so long as he can provide a reliable service. The need for timeliness is obvious with such operations as combining or hay baling but other jobs, such as hedge trimming or manure handling can cause loss of potential output, if as a result of their delay, ploughing, cultivations or the yarding of cattle cannot take place at the optimum time.

Before leaving the subject of additional labour inputs, the need for and part played by relief services should be mentioned. As the size of work force on many farms continues to decline and as holiday entitlement increases, the need to employ occasional help becomes more frequent. Agencies are in the business to meet such a need but difficulties do arise especially in the area of supervision of the short term employees. Some producers are overcoming the problem by forming groups so as to employ a regular person who carries out, in rotation, the relief duties for the members. So much for the acquisition of resources.

OPERATING THE PLAN

The third and most important part of production is the operation or implementation of the plan. It is all about getting the job done. It entails the organisation of resources – the most appropriate resources – so that they are in the right place at the right time. Once again, it involves many of those aspects of management discussed in the early chapters of the book, i.e. setting targets, planning, decision making, communicating and controlling – as applicable to the short term. Plans need to be frequently adjusted in order to account for outside influences such as weather conditions, market situations and disease outbreaks.

Production in the majority of farm situations does not mean just one straightforward job; it involves numerous differing operations which usually need to be carried out in a particular sequence, for example, drilling maize, rolling, followed by the application of pre-emergence herbicide. The critical job is the one upon which other jobs are dependent, and therefore has to be given priority. Ploughs need to be 'kept ahead' on heavy land in the autumn, as do pea cutters ahead of the viners; otherwise the whole operation comes to a halt if the critical job stops. Sharpening the blades of a precision chop forage harvester should, for instance, take place outside the normal shift so as not to hold up the remainder of the team. In some circumstances, it may be advantageous to put a temporary halt to the main job, to enable others to catch up, so that subsequent ones which are less weather-dependent can be carried out if weather conditions change. On a small farm, the combine harvester, for example, can be justifiably stopped for a short period to enable straw to be baled and carted so that stubble cultivating can take place if and when rain occurs. Such a hold-up in combining can be built into a cereal cropping system with a proportion of the crop in winter sown barley. It is possible to take advantage of the break in combining before other varieties are ripe to clear straw and begin seed bed preparations for drilling oil seed rape. In large scale organisations, it may be possible to have a number of jobs taking place simultaneously, but on the average-sized holding, as the gang size is reduced such an opportunity is less likely, so that sequencing of jobs becomes even more important.

Short term decision making is a key function in a situation where one operation has to follow another at a very precise time, as with the forage harvester picking up a wilted swath for ensiling into a tower. As the dry matter of the chopped material is so critical, management decisions need to be taken on the spot, involving frequent sampling and subsequent control particularly to the rate of work of the cutting machinery.

Although many jobs have to be carried out in sequence, each one is a separate operation and the rate of work does not directly affect the others, as, for example, with ploughing, cultivating and drilling. On the other hand, there are many other operations such as silage making and most systems of root harvesting, where several jobs link closely together and where overall output is determined by one particular job with lowest output. Selection of equipment of appropriate size and throughput will minimise such problems, but length of haul or abnormal soil conditions will put a system out of balance and may justify the input of additional, although temporary, resources at any bottleneck point. This is yet another example of the need for management, perhaps in such a case a foreman, to be 'out and about' adjusting the flow of resources as circumstances change. He could perhaps drive an additional transport vehicle which still allowed him to be regularly in the field and back at the store supervising both ends of the operation. The availability of stand-by equipment and essential items such as spare wheels and replacement hydraulic hose can have a marked effect on throughput, not only in a direct way but also indirectly through the motivation of operators responding to the confidence of having an efficient 'back-up' service.

So much of arable and livestock production involves moving materials from one point to another so that transport management is an important component of a manager's job. Managers of large-scale industrial operations commonly use the technique of **critical path analysis** which pinpoints bottlenecks and indicates how best to move resources and keep vital jobs moving. Few situations in farming necessitate such a formal approach, but the principle of detailed thinking, planning and action is what efficient day-to-day farm management is about.

In farming systems involving a number of enterprises, the problem frequently arises where several jobs should be done at the same time. The making of first-cut silage often clashes with shearing in a dairy and sheep situation, as does spraying with a wide range of jobs on the arable farm. Priorities have therefore to be made and perhaps calculations undertaken to indicate which is the most profitable or critical job. If this becomes a regular problem, then some change to the system may be required such as the use of a different variety, sowing date or even a change of enterprise.

Many of the examples quoted above, refer to field and cropping situations but the operation of livestock enterprises involves similar and in many situations, additional considerations. Animals respond well to routine, so that particularly feeding and milking need to be given priority and other tasks fitted into the day as and when convenient. Short diversions from the main task may be sensible in certain circumstances as alternative methods of dealing with the problem would be too expensive. In the small dairy herd, milking will just have to wait if a difficult calving occurs. In the large herd, the early morning milker can fulfil a valuable role in checking the calving cows before starting to milk. He may even spend a limited time assisting a cow in difficulty but then help must be soon called as considerable milk will be lost by further delay to the main job. Routine tasks, especially in an intensive livestock unit, take up a considerable part of the working day so that it is with some difficulty that other essential, but less routine, jobs have to be carried out. Machinery servicing, building and equipment maintenance are perhaps the best examples of jobs that tend to have a low priority with many stockmen. Naturally and correctly, the animals come first, but constant neglect of other tasks soon leads to inefficiencies. In these circumstances, managers have to effect control, by providing perhaps short term assistance, to 'wind up' the system and demonstrate how jobs can be carried out more easily if machinery and equipment are well maintained.

None of the issues so far discussed are important in their own right but only in so far as they become subsequently reflected in overall performance. Achieving the objectives of the business involves implementation of the plans which lead to the achievement of previously specified levels of performance. Let us consider, for example, a dairy farmer aiming to calve his replacement heifers at two years of age. In order to achieve the target weight and condition at calving, it is essential to keep the heifers growing well at every stage, as there is just no time for store periods. This involves regular weighing and comparison with targets so that corrective action can be taken in good time. Control of performance is less difficult when the animals are housed, as rapid adjustments can take place to diet or to the environment. It is in the grazing animal that growth rate problems arise, caused by weather conditions, which affect the animals directly and indirectly through forage quality and availability. Standards of husbandry and of grassland management are therefore key factors in sustaining animal performance. Decisions and actions have to be taken on a daily basis in respect of such factors as: nitrogen fertiliser application, movement to alternative grazing or the need to provide supplementary feed. It also involves making judgements as to the expected growth of forage in the weeks ahead.

Plans are made and decisions taken so that satisfactory performance is achieved. Naturally, things often go wrong, and this may be an appropriate point to mention the subject of uncertainty. Uncertainty affects the short term considerations of operating a farm just as it does the long term. Yields and prices are subject to uncertainty, but so is the important practical aspect of getting the job done. A wet autumn not only reduces the available days to operate machinery, but it also reduces the rate of work, when machines can get onto the land. In many farming situations, it may be justifiable to expect that the desired level of performance can be obtained in seven or eight years out of ten. This may be satisfactory, in respect of such considerations as combine harvester capacity in relation to the acreage of cereals to be harvested, as in the difficult years additional capacity can be hired. However, when rearing dairy heifers to calve at two years of age, such uncertainty will be unacceptable. As well-grown animals are such an important input into dairy farming, it may only be acceptable to deal with smaller heifers one year out of ten. In such an occasional circumstance, it may be possible to minimise the number of animals joining the herd by a temporary reduction in the culling rate of older cows. In order to reduce the uncertainty of obtaining low growth rates at pasture, availability of forage should not be a limiting factor, so that stocking rates should allow for this with surplus material, in the good growing years, being taken off for conservation. With the continued development of mechanised feeding and manure handling systems, it is expected that there will be a trend away from grazing replacement heifers as, in 'confinement' systems, growth rates will be more readily controlled. There are practical and technical ways of contending with uncertainty which supplement the initial choice of enterprises and methods of marketing that managers use to reduce the risks that are an inherent part of the industry.

One remaining point that needs to be considered in respect to operating the farm plan, is the question of supervision. It will be mentioned again in Chapter 10 but cannot be overlooked here. As we have seen, the manager's task is to see that jobs get done on time and to appropriate standards. It involves ensuring that members of staff understand what is expected of them, why the job is necessary and the reasons for doing it in a particular way. Ideally, they will have been involved in setting targets for the particular job, they will have the appropriate tools and other resources, and need then to be left to get on with the task in hand.

Managers should be available as and when required to assist with the supply of additional resources such as spare parts or extra seed to complete the drilling of a field. Older and more experienced members of staff need less supervision whereas the younger trainees require help, advice and encouragement, in order to build confidence. Supervision involves knowing when things are in order – but also knowing when they are not – and in knowing what best to do to correct things whether by more careful guidance and watchfulness over staff or by intervening in a way that actually redirects operations and resources.

SOME QUESTIONS RELATING TO THIS CHAPTER

(1) At what point can you be said to have produced a commodity?
(2) Which of the methods of planning a production programme described in this chapter is most appropriate to your circumstances?
(3) How important a part of a manager's job do you consider the procuring of resources to be?
(4) 'Timeliness is a major factor in the successful management of every farm'. Do you agree? Are there exceptions?
(5) How do you deal with uncertainty in your business?
(6) Are some farm enterprises easier to supervise than others? What are the problems with the difficult ones?

A GUIDE TO SELECTED FURTHER READING

Drucker, P. F. 1968. *The Practice of Management*. London: Heinemann; London: Pan Books.
Chapter 9 sets the scene on production.

Lowe, P. H. 1970. *The Essence of Production*. London: Pan Books.
Unusually, this book really is about production.

Green, J. R. 1978. How I Manage my Business. *Farm Management* **3,** no. 9, 407–12.
This article describes just what the author says it does; an unusually simple and helpful statement about what he is trying to produce and achieve.

Barnard, C. S. and J. S. Nix 1973. *Farm Planning and Control*. Cambridge: Cambridge University Press.
Chapter 1, pp 10–13; a condensed but comprehensive statement about uncertainty.

8
Buying and selling

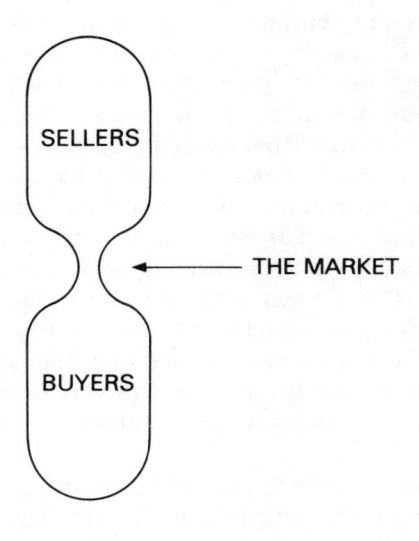

```
      SELLERS
         │
         ├──── THE MARKET
         │
      BUYERS
```

AN ECONOMIC VIEW

If production, as a subject, has its complexities, then marketing cannot be far behind. Indeed, there is evidence from research findings that many farmers and managers find the whole subject of marketing one of the most perplexing that confronts them. It is not that they do not know how to buy and sell – on the contrary, many of them are very adept at those two things – it is that a clear view of marketing, as a discipline, and of their individual role in it, often eludes them. They are frequently urged, from professional and political platforms and from the farming press, to 'improve their marketing', a plea that sometimes leaves them even more confused, and asking themselves, 'just what does that mean; what can I do that I am not already doing?'. We cannot, in one short chapter, pretend to be able to answer that question in any detail even if we had the knowledge applicable to the marketing of all agricultural commodities. Instead, therefore, we have chosen to offer a general view of marketing which may help readers to understand the subject a little better and to see more clearly where they personally stand in relation to it.

First, we wish, as we did in the last chapter, to refer briefly to a simple economic concept: this time it is 'utility'. In economic terms (and we cannot, in any activity which is concerned with resource-use, get too far away from them) utility means the power of a commodity or service to give satisfaction by meeting a need. This means that from the point of view of the consumer, nothing has been finally produced until it has reached the point where it can be purchased and can actually yield satisfaction. Milk, for instance, has not been finally produced until it is on the household table. Potatoes have not been produced until they are in the hands of the consumer, and even then there is some domestic processing to be undertaken before they can literally be consumed. The commercial processes that help to *present* commodities to the housewife are therefore as much part of the overall production process as the primary production process itself.

All of this means that although, for practical purposes, it is convenient to think of production and marketing as two separate kinds of activity, they are, in fact, all part of the same continuous process of bringing raw materials to the point where they have utility for the consumer. Many writers on the subject would take this view quite firmly and it results in marketing being placed alongside production, at the forefront of all industrial activity. Nothing should be produced that is not wanted by somebody else; and that is why we made specific reference to the requirements of the market in our definition of management in Chapter 2.

Seen in this light the farmer, while performing a vital early stage in the production–marketing process, is simply one link in a very long chain – albeit one of the earliest links and one without which the others would not exist. In this broad view of things, virtually all of a farmer's decisions – especially the major ones relating to his farming programme of the kind that were discussed in the previous chapter – can be seen, ultimately, as marketing decisions as well as production decisions. They help to determine what kind of a link in the total chain he will provide. To this extent, no matter how perplexing the subject of marketing appears to him, and no matter how uninvolved or helpless 'to improve his marketing' any individual farmer feels, he is, in fact, involved. He cannot avoid being so. The fact that he is in business ensures it and he cannot opt out.

THE FARMER'S DILEMMA

Whilst there may be many farmers and farm managers who would not disagree with this economic view of marketing, there are many who, nevertheless, feel in something of a dilemma in this area of their business. The dilemma is this: on the one hand they recognise the inevitability of their involvement; they do, after all, have to buy and sell. They are also aware that, as they seek opportunities to improve or to maintain profit levels, no area of their businesses – and certainly not a major one like marketing – should be ignored. After all, in the systematic approach to reviewing adjustment possibilities, set out in the last chapter, the first kind of possibility concerned increasing gross margins from individual enterprises – and one approach to that could be through seeking better prices for the same commodity or for an improved version of it. No stone should be left unturned and no obvious avenue left unexplored. Farmers with this frame of mind undoubtedly feel the urge to get further involved in the production – marketing chain.

On the other hand, those same farmers often see marketing as a highly professional, commercialised activity conducted – in comparison with the number of agricultural producers and the even larger number of consumers – by a relatively small number of firms and people; hence the hourglass image at the front of this chapter. It would be difficult to try to compete with them; not even sensible; so, in the interests of a good division of labour, why try to? Why not concentrate, they say to themselves, on the farmer's *real* job: that of physical production. That would surely be getting the priorities right, and all managers are urged to do that.

A POSSIBLE ANSWER

Both of these views are understandable, sensible and probably right. We believe that any working answer to the marketing dilemma, as we have described it, will require an acceptance of that view and an acceptance of the compromises that follow from it. The precise answer for any individual will, as we shall see, depend on the nature of his business and his own attitude to it. The main purpose of this chapter is to encourage individuals to develop and recognise what their attitude is.

A major part of the compromise will be to accept that, to a considerable extent, the two apparently conflicting attitudes towards marketing that we have described are, in fact, both tenable, and that, in a narrowly professional sense, marketing is something best left to the professionals. It involves them in such specialised matters as market research, product identification, the exploration of distribution channels, merchandising, price fixing and advertising, a highly technical and commercial set of activities which really are unlikely to concern most farmers or farm managers very much. Such activities tend to be located towards the consumer end of our chain of production and the average farmer – there will, of course, be exceptions – is unlikely to have the kind of interest, expertise or necessary commercial backing, to make it sensible for him to try to compete in marketing in this sense.

As we have already noted, however – hence the title of this chapter – the farmer is *very* much involved in the straightforward business of buying and selling. He owes it to his business to try to be as effective in these areas as he tries to be in the more practical farming areas. To put it bluntly, when a farmer wants to get hold of some spares for a broken machine or when he is trying to decide when to off-load some of his grain harvest, he is well and truly involved in the business of marketing. It involves him in both buying and selling. Both activities involve him in the market – even if the telephone or some other modern means of communication has, for the most part, taken over from the rituals of the traditional market place.

Marketing then, first, in the sense that it is part and parcel of the overall productive process and secondly, because it involves buying as well as selling, should be an important part of any farmer's thinking and activity, alongside the various other aspects of management that are discussed in this book. It has little to do with those specialised aspects of the marketing profession in which most farmers would be ill advised to try to compete and probably would not wish to. Let us therefore now take a brief look at those two parts of the subject in which they do have to compete.

BUYING

We have placed buying before selling partly to emphasise that marketing is not confined only to selling and partly because, of the two activities, it is likely to occupy most time. The importance of selling produce on satisfactory terms cannot, of course, be over emphasised, but for most farming enterprises and commodities their sale is not a continuous flow, but a series of separate sales, sometimes limited to one or two transactions a year, following a harvest. On the other hand the purchase of the many resources that are required in order to farm, will, depending on the system of farming, tend to be incurred much more frequently and much more variously.

The practical aspects of acquiring different kinds of resources have already been discussed in the previous chapter, as part of the production scene. We shall, therefore, satisfy ourselves here with some general comment about the principles involved. We suggest that, basically, there are six requirements that should be met:

(a) That the commodity or requisite purchased will meet, in a physical way, the need it was intended to, i.e. that it will do the job in question.
(b) That the purchase will not only do the job but will meet whatever level of quality is required, either in terms of eventual produce, i.e. crops and livestock, or in terms of a task undertaken, i.e. a repair, or alteration to buildings or machinery.
(c) That purchase can be made at a competitive price, given that the first two requirements are met, and that payment can be made at a mutually acceptable time.
(d) That, where it is appropriate, some assurance of continued and prompt service can be guaranteed by the supplier.

(e) That transactions can be made on a continuing basis, with the maintenance of goodwill on both sides.
(f) That satisfaction can be achieved without an undue use of time and effort.

Remembering the simile of the hourglass, farmers will usually be buying in a market – especially at the local level – that has a relatively small number of merchants and suppliers, each probably with more commercial power than any of the individual farmers buying from them. It is in these circumstances that farmers must decide, again, what kind of a link they wish to be in the production–marketing chain. Do they wish to buy as individuals or to become part of a group or co-operative body, accepting the discipline of that body, but also enjoying any of the commercial expertise and power that it will undoubtedly acquire? Bearing in mind that part of his requirements will be to have an assured service with goodwill and without undue effort, it should not be assumed that a small number of suppliers – conjuring up, as it does, the image of the middle man – is necessarily a disadvantage. In many ways, not least in terms of effort, it may be a considerable advantage, but it is for each individual purchaser to decide how he deals with those suppliers; in particular, whether alone or with others.

SELLING

A word or two now about selling. What we wish to say under this heading follows directly from our contention that the dividing line between production and marketing is a thin one, if it really exists at all. Basically, we see three different kinds of selling decisions that confront a farmer:

First, at the risk of labouring the point, there are decisions that will more usually be thought of as production decisions, but which have obvious and unavoidable marketing implications. When decisions are made about *what* commodities to produce, decisions are, in effect, being made about *what* will be sold and to whom. When a decision is made about *when* to produce (e.g. summer or winter milk), a decision is also being made about *when* to sell, and of course about what costs to incur and what sort of price to accept. When decisions are being made about what *quality* of goods to produce (e.g. feed or malting barley) then, again, marketing implications ensue relating to different sectors of the market. All of these considerations are directly linked to two of the economic concepts that we have dwelt upon earlier: *effective demand* in the last chapter and *utility* in this one. No farmer will presumably make decisions to produce anything without good reason to believe that enough individuals will collectively express their *effective demand* with money because the commodity in question provides them with *utility*. Perhaps what is implied, more than anything else, when farmers are urged to improve their marketing is simply that they should be more aware of these consumer considerations.

Secondly, farmers must decide what kinds of outlets they will use for their produce. Sometimes, in some countries, the commodity itself will determine this for them (e.g. in the UK, milk via the Milk Marketing Board) but frequently a choice will exist: choice in terms of physical outlets and choice in terms of time, i.e. whether to use spot sales or some form of forward contract. Much will still depend on the type of product, and on the attitude of the individual farmer towards considerations of risk.

Finally, we revert to the question, 'what kind of link in the chain?'. Each farmer will have to decide whereabouts he wishes to be in the chain and whether he wishes to be a link on his own or to act co-operatively with others. Does he wish to limit his involvement in marketing and concentrate his efforts largely on production? Does he wish to get nearer to the consumer, say, at the farm gate, or in some form of commercially integrated activity? Does he wish to go it alone or accept the advantages, and disadvantages, of combined effort? How many eggs in fact, does he wish to have in how many baskets? What, in fact, are the possibilities that are open to him? These are the questions he should ask himself and to which he should seek answers.

EXAMPLES OF SELLING

Some of the possibilities that confront the farmer in this context are now demonstrated in two examples. Two contrasting farm enterprises will be taken to illustrate the range of producer involvement in the marketing function: store lambs from a hill farm, where the normal involvement is minimal; and ware potatoes from an arable holding, where the opportunities are numerous.

First, we consider the marketing of *store lambs from a hill farm* where by custom, the annual crop of male and surplus female lambs are sold at specially arranged local sales, on one or more days during the early autumn months. The returns from the crop of lambs are a major component of the producer's annual income, this being supplemented by compensatory allowances (formerly hill subsidies), wool and the sale of draft ewes. Unfortunately, for the hill farmer, his influence on lamb income is limited as factors beyond his control not only determine prices but also the numbers available for sale, their size, condition and even the time of selling.

The harsh physical environment of the typical hill farm with its high elevation, exposure, cold, wet winters, short growing seasons and acidic soils offers little in the way of alternative enterprises. These conditions determine to a considerable extent: flock size, breed of ewe, lambing date as well as numbers reared and rates of growth. Time of selling has to be carefully matched to forage supplies, with reduction in stock numbers taking place before summer growth is completed, so as to leave sufficient forage on the swards to provide keep for the breeding flock during the winter months. Skill in stockmanship and manipulation of the limited resources is reflected in the numbers and the quality of lambs available for sale, but these environmental factors – particularly the weather conditions – have a marked effect on annual income.

The lambs are purchased by lowland farmers for fattening during the winter and early spring months, a high proportion being fattened in arable areas on catch crop roots or arable by-products. The price these farmers are prepared to pay for store lambs is influenced by the returns they expect to receive for the fattened animals as well as by such factors as the growth of root crops and cash availability which is influenced to a considerable extent by yields and prices of other arable crops.

The hill farmer does get considerable satisfaction from selling his lambs at the annual sales, especially in the years when he has a good crop. The occasion is a highlight of the farm year when he competes with his neighbours (who have experienced similar weather conditions) to obtain a prize card as well as a good price for his lambs. To some older and well established breeders, the prize card can produce just as much satisfaction as the financial returns.

Developments in the marketing of hill lambs are taking place, instigated by producers with financial objectives very much to the forefront. These take the form of producer groups or individual hill farmers forming a closer business relationship with a lowland farm. Members of a marketing group are able to 'pool' their animals and form larger batches of matching lambs to meet the requirement of individual buyers. One of the members with time, skill and particularly a marketing interest can develop contracts, arrange transport and hopefully provide a service to buyers so that the overall returns are improved. Farmers joining such a group need to appreciate the fact that, in a year of depressed prices, their returns may well be an improvement over those obtained from traditional selling, but in the good years there could possibly be little or no financial benefit from co-operation. Longer term advantages of grouping such as breed improvement schemes, progeny testing and bulk buying have been shown to assist group loyalty.

Individual hill farmers keen to be more involved in the marketing chain are integrating their breeding enterprise with that of a fattening enterprise on a lowland farm. Lambs are transferred at a mutually convenient time with an interim payment being made. Partial ownership is retained until the animals are slaughtered, when the returns are shared on a previously agreed basis. Such a system provides a more equitable return to the breeder and the fattener should have healthier lambs, which have received appropriate preventative medicinal treatments, as against unnecessary time and money being spent on making them look attractive for the store sales. Breeders can, with such a system, follow the progeny of individual rams through to slaughter and by selection, improve the type and value of their output. The integration can expand, for instance, by transferring hay, straw or concentrates in the lorries which are used to collect lambs. Summering of lowland stock on the hill pastures and lowland wintering of ewe lamb replacements are other possible joint schemes.

These developments clearly demonstrate the close relationship between the production and marketing functions and in the hill farm situation where non-management factors can have a significant influence on returns, these can be improved by diverting effort and skills along the marketing chain.

The second example we consider is the producer of *ware potatoes* who is to some extent in a similar position to the hill farmer having a product to sell with quantity and quality markedly influenced by weather conditions and with price levels outside his control. On the other hand, a potato grower has numerous alternative courses of action available to him in production to improve his returns from the market. He can, soil type, rotations and quotas permitting, vary the size of enterprise to match a particular market outlet, e.g. a local retail shop. The variety, planting date and seed rate can be varied to meet the requirement of the market. Other techniques used for this purpose include seed sprouting, irrigation, harvesting method and particularly those involved with storage.

Specialist producers of early potatoes have the least influence on their returns, being considerably dependent upon weather conditions and on prices being paid at the time they need to lift the crop. The management, and economy, of many such holdings is dependent upon the timely planting of a following broccoli crop so that when the potatoes have bulked to a reasonable level, lifting and immediate sale of this perishable product has to take place – regardless of price. Shopping around to find a buyer offering the best price on the day is a worthwhile exercise providing that nothing is sacrificed in terms of service in collection or in prompt payment.

Second early varieties can be lifted if the market demands or they can be left in the ground to mature if later selling appears to be more attractive. It is the grower of main crop varieties who has the widest choice of marketing alternatives: from selling in the field at 'spot' prices; wholesale; retail or even 'pick your own'; to contract selling throughout the year from specialist storage facilities. The nearer he gets to the consumer, the more important will visual appearance and cooking quality of the product be. Further sales from a farm shop or similar retail outlet relying on regular customers can be jeopardised by marketing an inferior product if only for a short period of time. Regulations requiring the registered number of a grower to be printed on every sack should in the long term keep inferior potatoes off the market, but, in the meantime and especially in years of undersupply, there is usually a buyer to be found – 'at a price'.

Co-operative marketing has not developed to the same extent with potatoes as with many other farm products. Likely reasons for this are the widely fluctuating prices from year to year and as with the store lamb groups, member loyalty is a problem at periods of short supply. Tuber quality also varies from one season to another even with the same varieties, seed source, and soil type. Producers who develop and use husbandry techniques which aid reliability of quality, rather than those which maximise yield, should in the future be increasingly rewarded by price. If a system of quantifying tuber quality can be developed perhaps even specifying suitability for a particular market, e.g. chipping or roasting, then producers will no doubt take a greater interest in the marketing of their crop.

MARKET INTELLIGENCE

The final part of this chapter, apart from a brief conclusion, considers the question of market intelligence data and the part that they may or may not play in marketing decisions.

The major difficulty, as we see it, about all such decisions in farming is that they have to be made at a given point of time in respect to circumstances that will exist at some future point in time. This arises because of the length of the production cycle and because of the generally long term nature of any commitment to specialise in the production of one or another agricultural enterprise. Capital and expertise quickly become relatively fixed – a problem which is at the root of all investment decisions, as we shall see in the next chapter.

It has been said that successful marketing means having the right commodity, at the right place, at the right price and at the right time. But decisions do have to be made *now* in order that this can be done *later on* – and, as we saw in the chapter on decision making, having information is an important part of that process. Some of the information that is necessary will relate to circumstances that already exist on the farm in question, for example, records of past (and therefore expected) physical performance levels. To this kind of information, however, will have to be added the best possible estimates that can be made of future prices and costs, both in the short and in the long term. A whole chapter has been devoted, towards the end of this book, to the matter of acquiring information, including market intelligence data. In the meantime, we see two fundamentally different kinds of decisions which have to be made, for which some indication of market circumstances may be helpful.

First, there are decisions about what enterprises to be in; whether to expand, or contract, whether to get in, or to get out. Such decisions are strategic in nature and tend not to be made too often – indeed, it may be dangerous if they are. Sometimes they are made for non-economic reasons, as, for instance, when an ageing farmer decides to quit a physically demanding enterprise like milk production. To the extent, however, that an eye must be kept on likely changes in effective demand, we think it wise for farmers and farm managers wherever they are, to keep reasonably abreast of any available 'situation' and 'outlook' material as well as responsible comment on such matters as national and international production trends and economic forecasts, not to mention political events, and relevant scientific and technical developments. We appreciate that this is a tall order. Much of this kind of information may not be readily available or readily quantifiable and, because of the inherent uncertainty and interactions of world affairs, may be overtaken by subsequent events. We do not believe that it would be wise for a farmer to use this kind of material to make hasty or constant changes to his farming systems and methods. We do, however, believe that he is likely to make better long term strategic decisions if he is informed about these matters rather than if he is not. If it only serves to convince him that he is doing the right things, and to encourage him to go on doing them as well as he can, it will have been an invaluable exercise.

The second kind of decision for which commercial information can be helpful is much shorter term. The farming press, local radio, producer organisations, personal observation and direct requests for information to the trade, may all be of help. The question here will not be related to the adjustment of enterprises or farm systems, but to the disposal of produce from existing enterprises. The fact that there is a choice – to dispose now or later – implies, of course, that we are concerned here either with non-perishable supplies or with livestock that may be 'taken on'. In a nutshell, the question to be answered is, 'does one sell (or buy) now or later?'. So far as selling is concerned there will usually be some cost of waiting: feeding stuffs, storage, interest charges, and, of course any other lost opportunities (economists talk, literally, about 'opportunity cost') from locked-up capital.

But there may also be gain from waiting in the form of higher prices. This is a situation for the use of a partial budget in which potential gains and potential losses can be weighed against each other. The word 'potential' has deliberately been used here because neither set of information – especially the returns – can be guaranteed. Nevertheless, *decisions have to be made*. It is impossible to defer indefinitely; remember, to do nothing is to do something. Sooner or later the best possible estimate must be made, and, as with longer term decisions, it is surely better to have some information, especially from the more reputable sources, than to have none. In the last resort, however, these are the questions on which farmers have to make their own judgements and they may rely as much on their intuitive 'feel' for situations as on any formal analysis of trends, however sophisticated or crude that may be. They also know that they cannot 'win' all the time, and they have a proper regard for goodwill and mutual trust.

In discussing both the outlook data relevant to longer term situations and shorter term market intelligence data we have carefully expressed the view that such information *may* help in the appropriate decision situations. We do not know that it *will*, and there is always the possibility that if too many make the right decision, their combined effect on supply and demand will be to make it the wrong one. We cannot allow ourselves, however, despite this threat, to believe that worse decisions are likely to be made when there is access to such information, compared with when there is not. What we do believe, is that good decisions do not automatically follow from having market information available, however good it may be. Good decisions embrace so much more.

CONCLUSION

At the outset of this chapter we made it clear that we did not intend to try to provide answers to individual marketing problems. We believe, however, that farmers and farm managers, many of them known to us, find the subject of marketing a perplexing one and that their own attitude is often unclear, if not inconsistent. We have, therefore, offered a series of thoughts intended to help individuals, first, to get the subject into some better perspective and, secondly, to see more clearly their own possible role within it. We would summarise those thoughts in this way:

First, that in the short term, farmers may be helped in their approach to marketing if they recognise:

(a) that they will not usually be *in* marketing in an 'aggressive' professional sense;
(b) that they are nevertheless *in* marketing whether they know it or not, and whether they like it or not;
(c) that all business decisions which relate to production (and sooner or later most of them do) are also marketing decisions;
(d) that room for manoeuvre in marketing is largely dictated by farming enterprises and by personal attitudes to independence and risk; but that even to recognise that there may not be much room for manoeuvre is to recognise a marketing reality;
(e) that buying goods and services is as much part of marketing as selling them, and that timely delivery can be vital;
(f) that a serious effort should be made by farmers to understand the structure, functions and services of those marketing institutions – government and commercial – with which they are concerned, whether in a commercial, regulatory or a developmental way:
(g) that all areas of a business should be explored in any endeavour to increase or improve profits and, depending on personal objectives and business circumstances, this may or may not include marketing. As a rule, it should; and as a rule it will be more helpful to have some information with which to help make decisions rather than not to have any.

Taking a long term view of this whole subject, we see a situation in which, for a good many years, the 'service' element in the economy has been increasing, and in which, with a growing division of labour, primary producers have become more and more removed from the final consumer. But we see also, at the time of writing, a growing desire (in the UK at least) on the part of farmers to become re-involved nearer to the point of the consumer. Farm shops, amongst other things, are evidence of this. It has always been true, however, that distant fields can look green and we wonder, as marketing in the professional sense becomes increasingly sophisticated and concentrated in large concerns, how much scope really exists for individual farmers to accept the opportunities and risks associated with this sector. Apart from 'marketing the environment', which they are uniquely placed to do, scope may well be limited to those (few?) who have the appropriate personal and commercial aptitudes and flair. This does not mean, however, that farmers are not and cannot be involved in marketing. The whole of this chapter, indeed, has been to suggest to the contrary. It may mean, however, that, for most in the industry, involvement will continue to be of a somewhat limited kind. Some, obviously, will be more involved than others. What *is* important is that *all* farmers should understand clearly what marketing role they do, can, and cannot play.

SOME QUESTIONS RELATING TO THIS CHAPTER

(1) To what extent do, or should, you think about marketing when you make production decisions?
(2) In thinking about a possible re-allocation of your time, should you devote more to on-the-farm production, or more to selling and buying?
(3) When did you last seriously review your marketing methods for each of your main farming enterprises?
(4) What real use do you make of situation and outlook reports, or market intelligence data?
(5) Can you, with good effect, involve yourself in marketing more directly to the final consumer?
(6) How much do you know about the principal organisations with which you deal when you buy and sell?

A GUIDE TO SELECTED FURTHER READING

Donaldson, J. G. S. and Frances Donaldson 1972. *Farming in Britain Today*. West Drayton, Middlesex: Penguin Books.
Chapters 4, 5 and 6 provide an invaluable account of the structure and function of many relevant organisations in the UK.
Beresford, T. 1975. *We Plough the Fields: Farming in Britain Today*. West Drayton, Middlesex: Penguin Books.
A well written book, worth reading in its entirety, but Part Four, especially, offers a perspective on agricultural trading and the future.
Bateman, D. I. (ed.) 1972. *Marketing Management in Agriculture*. Dept of Agricultural Economics, University College of Wales.

See also:

Farm Management, 1972, **2**, no.3; 1974, **2**, no.8 and 1975-6, **3**, no.1.
 Three issues of the Journal, each of which contains a number of helpful articles on marketing.
 Outlook and situation material published by various Universities, Colleges, Advisory and Business Houses.

9
Finance

Financial management involves:

	The past and the present	The future
Trading	RECORDS AND ACCOUNTS	BUDGETS
Capital	BALANCE SHEETS	INVESTMENT APPRAISAL

CAPITAL AND FARMING

In keeping with the central theme of this book, the purpose of this chapter is not to spell out in detail the mechanics of every known financial management technique and practice, but to comment on their meaning and use, in the context of farming. In that way, we hope to assist the reader to develop, if he has not already done so, an ordered view of what often looks like an uncharted jungle.

There is, quite definitely, something frightening about this subject. No farmer or manager needs to be told of its importance, but it is an aspect of farm management from which many tend to shy away. As one farmer said to us when asked why he co-operated in an annual farm accounts scheme, 'Because, whether I like it or not, once a year I have to sit down and discuss things that I might otherwise avoid'. There are various understandable reasons for this kind of attitude. Financial matters can be complicated; they involve mathematics, and, even at an elementary level, that can produce mental blockages for many of us. Terminology is not always clearly defined, especially in the hands of amateurs; it can be a barrier to communication rather than an aid. And, of course, figures, when they are accurate, sometimes present a cold and unpalatable truth, and who wants to come face to face with that too often?

As a first step in picking our way through this subject, it will perhaps help to recognise an essential difference between the way an economist regards capital and the way most businessmen do. To the economist, capital is one of three separate factors of production, together with land and labour. Each has its own characteristics and its reward. Capital, in this context, represents deferred consumption; a *stock* of resources produced in some previous time period, to be used to satisfy future wants, e.g. machinery, buildings, livestock, seeds and fertilisers, etc. To the average businessman, however, capital is something less precisely defined. It simply means the monetary value of his productive resources – whether he owns them or borrows the money to acquire them, and whether he uses them up on the spot or retains them. This is an absolutely reasonable view for him to take. We should keep it in mind, and it will help to eliminate some of the mystique that can otherwise surround the notion of capital. This simplified view of capital should also help to bring the subject right into the heart of practical farming itself, rather than to leave it as some sort of appendage to be nervous of. Using resources is, after all, what farm management is about. By definition, therefore – the businessman's definition, not the economist's – 'capital' equates with 'farming', and financial management is concerned with acquiring that capital, with using it and with maintaining it.

A WAY OF LOOKING AT FINANCIAL MANAGEMENT

We can now move on to look at the many and varied 'nuts and bolts' of which financial management is comprised. This could be approached in many different ways and there is nothing sacrosanct about the approach that we propose to adopt, except that it is simple. It is depicted in the two-way diagram at the beginning of the chapter. It is based on the simple assumption that the subject can be subdivided both in *content* and in *time* into two parts. So far as content is concerned there are: (a) those aspects of financial management that are to do with day-to-day *trading* activities, and (b) those that are more to do with the 'state of play' in the business at particular points of time, i.e. with its *capital* status. So far as time is concerned, there are: (a) considerations which relate to the *present and the recent past* (we find it difficult to differentiate between the two because the moment something happens it becomes part of the recent past), and (b) considerations which concern the *future*.

This view of things results in the four segments in our diagram. The top left-hand segment (recent and past trading) is primarily concerned with accounts and with the records that make them possible. The top right-hand segment (future trading) is concerned with various forms of budgets. Then turning to the capital side of things, the bottom left-hand segment (past capital) relates to balance sheets, while the bottom right-hand one concerns investment appraisal. Under each of these four headings (accounts, budgets, balance sheets and investment appraisal) there are numerous techniques and topics that make up the whole. Some of these issues have already been mentioned in other chapters. At the risk of some duplication, however, it seems necessary to comment here, even if very briefly, on all those aspects of the subject with which every farmer and farm manager should be reasonably conversant. This does not mean that he needs to be a financial wizard. But it does mean that he should have a *clear* view of what the relevant concepts and procedures mean, to the extent that in several of the more straightforward areas of the subject he should be capable of manipulating the relevant figures on his own. The itemised version of our diagram, below, indicates the particular topics that will be discussed.

	Past and present	Future
Trading	**ACCOUNTS** whole farm accounts (+ records) inputs and outputs comparative analysis gross margins net margins	**BUDGETS** complete partial break even and sensitivity cash flows
Capital	**BALANCE SHEETS** structure and meaning ratios return on 'existing' capital	**APPRAISAL** incremental capital rate of return pay back discounting investment checklist

SOME IMPORTANT OMISSIONS

Before proceeding, it should be said that there are certain important topics which, for reasons given in Chapter 1, have not been commented on. In particular this includes questions of company law and structure, and of taxation. Both topics require legal expertise which we do not have; they are shaped and influenced by particular national legislation and are subject, also, to constant change. In choosing to omit them we are not unmindful of their supreme importance, especially in the matter of maintaining business capital intact. We strongly advise all farmers and managers to employ, and cultivate, the appropriate professionals to advise them in these specialised matters. Such people are not commonly to be found amongst the general run of agricultural advisers and consultants. Very often, we fear, they are not easy to find amongst the more professional ranks either. There are many accountants, even in rural areas, for whom farmers constitute a relatively small share of their total custom and who seem to lack any deep expertise in farming finance. Too often, for instance, it seems to us that 'tax planning' boils down to the statement 'you look like making a good profit this year, what about replacing a tractor?' and too often farmers seem to be at the end of the queue for the speedy completion of accounts. The remedy, of course, is in their own hands, but that is another story.

ACCOUNTS

THE TRADING ACCOUNT

Interpreting a trading account is not as straightforward as it might appear. It is perhaps not too surprising, therefore, that we have met a number of farmers who are inclined to shy away from it. In fact, it does what its name implies, it gives an account of a year's trading. Strictly speaking a trading account and a profit and loss account are two different things, the former relating only to trading items directly associated with the main activity of the business in question, and the latter indicating final profit (or loss) after certain 'below the line' items of an overhead nature, have been taken into consideration. Very often, however, especially in small businesses, the terms are interchangeable and the niceties of terminology should not worry us here. What is important is what the account tells us, i.e. what profit or loss has been incurred and how it came about.

Profit, for any particular time period, is a measurement of the difference between the value of all the resources used in that time period, and the value of everything that was or could have been sold. To the extent that a business is a continuing operation, a trading account is rather like a slice out of a cake. Sturrock (see Further Reading) in what is still one of the best and most under-praised of the books on farm accounting, suggests that the notion is best understood by imagining that a farmer 'buys in' his valuation (from himself) on the opening day of the financial year and then continues to buy in resources during the year. He also sells produce during the year and 'sells out' the valuation (again to himself) on the last day. Opening and closing creditors and debtors must be taken into account, and profit, in this sense, is then the difference between *all selling and all buying*. In those countries where tax is based on profits, it will be based on this figure, even though a large part of it may be locked up in valuations; one day they will be released.

It is this basic understanding of what profit *means* that we wish to emphasise here. There are, however, two other important and, at first sight, rather confusing points to be added. First, it is in the nature of accountancy that no trading account can be guaranteed to be exactly accurate. In the preparation of accounts, conventions have to be employed to allow, for instance, for non-cash items like machinery depreciation, and for the valuation of produce and resources on hand. There is a tendency to be conservative in these matters so as not to anticipate profit that in the event may not accrue and, from time to time, conventions get changed. No farmer who has replaced machinery and equipment in recent years will be in any doubt about the realities of replacement cost, but accountants have yet to agree on how this and other similar issues should be dealt with in a uniform approach to 'inflation accounting' methods. There is, therefore, no such thing as an exactly true statement of profit; there is only a 'true and fair view'.

The second point concerns the difficulty of unravelling that true and fair view of things in order to make judgements about the efficiency – or lack of it – within the different sectors of a farm business. A trading account in its raw state is less help in this than might be imagined. There are two main reasons for this. First, the amount of detail shown in trading accounts is invariably inadequate; perhaps because inadequate records have been kept in the first place, perhaps because important items of cost or revenue, or of valuation have been lumped together by the accountant simply because there is no statutory need to give them in detail. Some of the calculations that one would like to make are, therefore, not possible without additional detail.

The second main difficulty in using a trading account for management purposes – i.e. for 'management accounting', as opposed to straightforward 'financial accounting' – is that in its normal format, information relating to particular enterprises or particular inputs is scattered throughout the document, some perhaps in the receipts, some in the expenditure and some in either of the valuations. The normal layout of a trading account is as follows:

Opening Valuation		Receipts
Expenses		Closing Valuation
Profit	or	Loss

It is virtually impossible to look at a trading account in this state – especially where livestock are involved – and to deduce, with any accuracy, what is happening. Some unravelling is required, some adjustments need to be made and some extra (physical) information introduced before we can talk about inputs and outputs and the efficiency with which the one is converted into the other.

INPUTS AND OUTPUTS

In order to fully understand the terms *input* and *output* we need to get away from the ideas of expenditure and sales. An input is the measure of how much of a resource is actually *used* in a given time period, whether or not it was paid for in that time period, or indeed, as in the case of family labour, whether it has an actual charge to it at all. Similarly, output is a measure of production in a given time period whether or not what was produced was actually sold. Valuations, at beginning and end, therefore form an important part of both concepts.

The conventional headings under which farm trading accounts are converted into statements of input and output, and the calculations involved are as follows:

Inputs	*Outputs*
(opening valuation + expenditure) minus (closing valuation)	(closing valuation + sales) minus (opening valuation + purchases)
Bought feed	Crops
Bought seed	Milk
Fertiliser	Cattle
Rent and rates	Sheep
Power and machinery	Pigs
Wages	Poultry
Sundries	Sundries

It is not our intention in this book (since it is readily available in others) to discuss in any detail either the arithmetic that is involved in this process or the kinds of recording and book keeping systems that are required in order to make this kind of analysis possible. Suffice to say that it all begins with the making of careful notes on the stubs of cheque books and bank paying-in books which should then be transferred into an appropriately headed cash analysis book.

In order, however, to arrive at the true measure of the total levels of output from each enterprise and the total quantity of inputs that have been absorbed by them, it must be remembered that the trading account does not necessarily tell the whole story. Quite apart from the falsifying effect of contra accounts – which must be carefully watched and allowed for – allowances may be needed for the transferance of items between enterprises (for example, the transfer of young stock from a breeding to a livestock rearing unit) which, so far as the trading account is concerned, simply do not appear. The extent to which such transfers need to be allowed for will depend on how fine a breakdown of enterprise output is required. There can, however, be no ignoring the fact that if cereals are grown and consumed by livestock on the farm, the cereals need to be credited and the food bill debited with the amount involved.

Coupled with a limited amount of basic physical information about the farm in question – its cropping and stocking, and, most important, an allocation of concentrated feed between livestock enterprises – these measurements of inputs and outputs can then be used in a variety of ways to test past performance and possible future decisions. Typical of such measurements would be outputs per productive unit (e.g. crop output per hectare, and livestock output per animal) and inputs per productive unit (e.g. food costs per £1 of output). In this way, raw financial data from the trading account – by itself not very helpful – can be transformed into useable management accounting data for use in 'account' and 'comparative' analysis which we now go on to discuss. We would encourage anyone who is managing a farm to try to become adept – if they are not already so – in the manipulation and interpretation of accounting data in this way.

COMPARATIVE ANALYSIS

Comparative analysis is the name generally given to the technique of comparing the financial results from one farm with average results drawn from a group of similar farms.

The main criticisms of comparative analysis in the past have been that no two farms are alike, that averaged results on a sample of farms (however similar) do not represent any real situation at all, and that management decisions are concerned with the effect of marginal adjustments within individual enterprises rather than with averaged results over the whole farm.

We would accept these criticisms in strict academic terms. In the real world, however, fairly crude tools are often necessary. We would defend a limited use of the technique on the grounds that averages do provide an indication of the level towards which results in any given population will tend; that it is natural for individuals to wonder where they stand in relation to that average, and that, unless in totally untutored hands, the general questioning of performances prompted by this exercise is unlikely to be other than beneficial. It is also true, however, that if judgements about performance are to be made at all – and how can that be avoided? – some form of comparison must inevitably be made against some known yardstick. Where that yardstick can be derived from established knowledge of technical performance levels within individual enterprises, all well and good. Where, however, whole-farm judgements are required, yardsticks or 'standards' are unlikely to be available other than from whole-farm financial surveys of the kind used in comparative analysis.

It is, of course, important that when such comparisons are made 'like' is compared with 'like' and that, conceptually, the calculations have meaning. In order to ensure that like is being compared with like, certain adjustments have to be made to trading account data before inter-farm comparisons can be made. In particular, allowances need to be made for the value of any unpaid labour that is being employed, and distortions resulting from variations in ownership charges (rents, mortgages, interest, etc.) must be avoided. In order for calculations to be meaningful, they must involve inputs and outputs that are logically related to each other. For example, milk output per cow, has meaning;

so does, milk output per hectare devoted to dairying, and sheep output per ewe, pig output per sow, wheat output per hectare of wheat, fertiliser use per hectare, and labour and machinery costs per hectare. All of these examples are conceptually meaningful in that the output figures have been related to the units (either livestock or land) from which they have been derived, and the input figures have been related to the units which absorb them. By contrast, input : output ratios make no sense when the dividend and the divisor have no logical relationship; when, for example, the output from one enterprise, occupying *part* of a farm, is expressed per hectare of the *whole* farm (e.g. sheep output per hectare of the whole farm, when they occupy only part of it) or when an input is not properly related to the production unit that absorbs it (e.g. concentrated feed per hectare, instead of per consuming livestock unit). If these kinds of calculations are used in comparative analysis the technique, not unnaturally, falls into disrepute.

There are obvious dangers that can arise on any particular farm from examining individual efficiency measures of this type in isolation, and from drawing too many conclusions without reference to the rest of the farm's economy. Ideally one would wish to examine all inter-related measures simultaneously, but in practice this is clearly not possible. One has to start somewhere. We suggest that a logical starting point is to begin with the profit; that, after all, is the main purpose of the exercise. Using the kind of sequence illustrated below one could then move on to consider those aspects of the farm where adjustment may be most possible, looking first at those factors which effect overall production levels (yields, prices and system intensity) and then at the more adjustable items of cost (feedingstuffs, labour and machinery). If the data being examined is cast in gross margin and fixed cost terms, the procedure to be followed need not differ in essence from this one.

Too often, we feel, this type of systematic analysis is reserved for situations in which profits have disappointed, when it could usefully be applied, as a routine tool of financial management. No one would want to claim for comparative analysis that it is a sophisticated tool, without its limitations. But neither would many, who have worked in the field as management advisers, grasping often at any reasonable straws, wish to reject it as a tool they will never use.

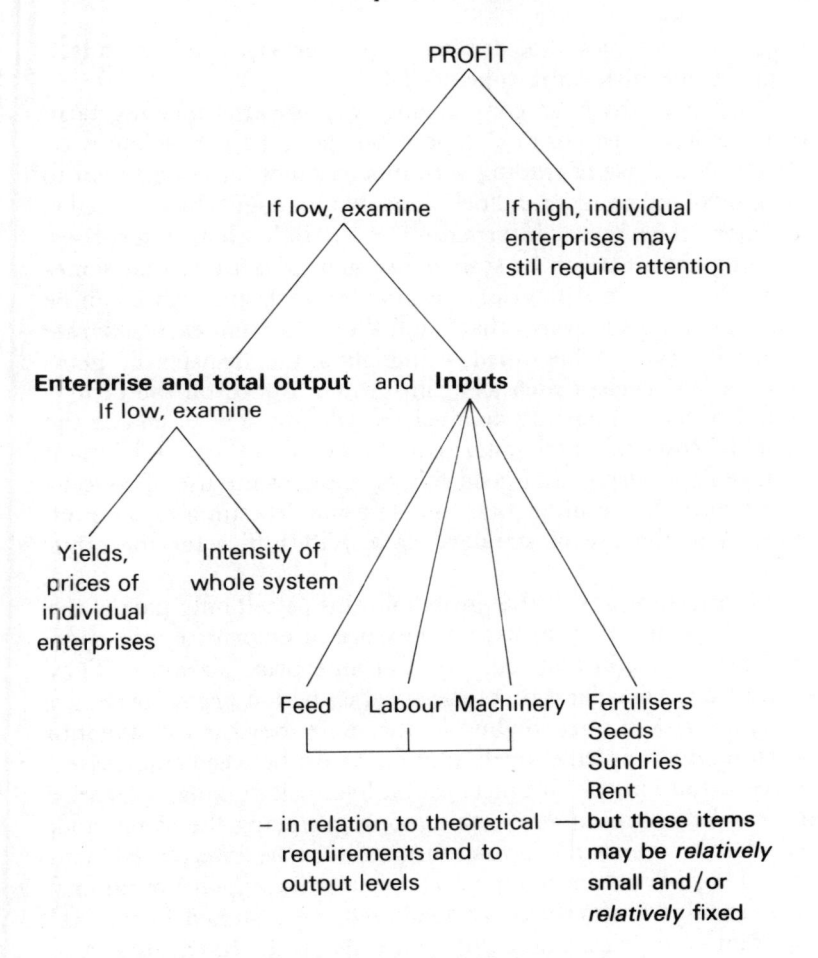

```
                            PROFIT
                           /      \
                          /        \
                  If low, examine   If high, individual
                     /    \         enterprises may
                    /      \        still require attention
                   /        \
                  /          \
Enterprise and total output  and  Inputs
   If low, examine                  /|\
      /    \                       / | \
     /      \                     /  |  \
    /        \                   /   |   \
 Yields,    Intensity of        /    |    \
 prices of  whole system       /     |     \
 individual                   /      |      \
 enterprises                 /       |       \
                          Feed   Labour  Machinery   Fertilisers
                          |_____|_____|        Seeds
                                   |                 Sundries
                                                     Rent
                     – in relation to theoretical — but these items
                        requirements and to          may be *relatively*
                        output levels                small and/or
                                                     *relatively* fixed
```

ENTERPRISE ACCOUNTS

Before moving on to consider the budgeting section of this whole subject, it is appropriate, at this point, to offer brief comment on the subject of enterprise accounts. We use the word 'accounts' deliberately rather than 'costs' so as not to confuse what we have in mind with full enterprise costings traditionally undertaken in many countries by agricultural economists, principally to provide evidence for price fixing discussions. So far as the farm manager is concerned that approach is likely to be more detailed than is necessary and because of the arbitrariness with which shared costs are sometimes allocated between enterprises, may even lead to positively misleading conclusions.

Gross margins have gone a long way towards meeting farm management needs in this respect, but perhaps not all the way. Certainly the use of trading accounts becomes more pertinent to the kind of judgements and decisions that managers have to make, the more they reveal information about individual enterprises. Trading accounts can be sufficiently manipulated so that something close to the true gross margins for each enterprise can be calculated. This requires that the full output from each separate enterprise can be identified – including the transfer of items between enterprises such as grain grown to feed on the farm – and also that sufficiently detailed records are kept to enable the variable costs of each enterprise to be identified. The main requirement here is that good records exist of the use of concentrated feed. More often than not reasonable estimates, or even a resort to the use of standard data, will suffice for the other items.

It is a fact, however, that gross margins do tell only part of the story. Although they provide a measure of enterprise efficiency, they are, by definition, only partial enterprise accounts. They exclude any consideration of the fixed costs that are absorbed by the enterprise in question and furthermore they cannot take into account any complementarity that may exist between enterprises; the contribution, for instance, that a livestock grazing enterprise may make to subsequent arable crops occupying the same land. All of this means that gross margins must be interpreted with care. They have their definite use; they also have their limitations. In particular it should be remembered, on a mixed farm, that different enterprises make different calls on the fixed costs. Any notion that fixed costs can be equally and meaningfully spread over the whole land area of a farm and that the gross margin from each enterprise should then be expected to cover that cost, is both false and misleading. There are obvious examples amongst the less intensive grassland enterprises, where a low gross margin per hectare is entirely acceptable on the grounds that it is the best available use for the area, makes few demands on the fixed costs, and may provide added fertility for extractive enterprises that follow.

It is largely because of a desire to understand more about the deployment of fixed costs that some farmers and managers have recently been seeking to develop enterprise accounts beyond the gross margin stage, towards the so-called net margin. By allocating some of the lumpy and easily allocatable fixed costs, as well as the variable ones, net margins can be produced that can be helpful in the following ways:

(a) They indicate *why* the fixed costs are being incurred, *where* they are being absorbed, and may prompt their *more economic deployment*.
(b) They indicate how overall farm profit has been built up.
(c) They provide the basis of the calculations that are required, if the elimination of a whole enterprise, as opposed to a marginal reduction or expansion, is being contemplated.

The framework for this kind of enterprise account is as follows:

	For whole enterprise	*Per hectare*
Enterprise output less variable costs	————	————
= Gross margin less allocatable fixed costs such as specialised machinery, labour and sundries	————	╲╱ ╳ ╱╲
= Net margin	————	

Although we believe that, properly interpreted, this kind of calculation is of value on a *whole enterprise basis*, we strongly urge that it should not be expressed on a per hectare basis. That figure could only relate to the *existing* scale of the enterprise in question and would be misleading when contemplating subsequent marginal changes in scale. It is the very lumpiness of the fixed costs that results in them being spread more thinly or thickly over an enterprise according to its scale. Different answers would emerge with every variation in scale. It is the strength of the measure we term the gross margin that it does not behave in this way. That is what makes it so helpful as a means of exploring the likely effect of marginal changes. Nevertheless we see an increasing interest in the net margin concept and, provided it stops short of trying to allocate items of cost that are not logically allocatable and provided it is interpreted carefully, we believe this to be reasonable.

BUDGETS

We turn now to the second of the four segments into which this Finance chapter has been divided. It concerns future trading and the preparation of budgets. There are four main kinds of budget which will be of most value in the management of a farm: complete budgets, partial budgets, break even and sensitivity budgets, and cash flows. The first two have already been touched upon, in the chapters on Control and Decision Making. They can, therefore, be dealt with briefly.

COMPLETE BUDGETS

In addition to providing a basis for budgetary control, complete budgets will be useful when:

(a) A new farm is being tendered for or taken over.
(b) When the system of farming on an existing farm is being so radically altered that a partial budget is inadequate to test the alternative systems.
(c) Simply as an essential indicator at the beginning of each year, of the kind of profit that is likely to be obtained from the existing farming system.

In our experience, the greatest difficulty in preparing all budgets, of whatever kind, is not *how* to calculate them in the mechanical sense, but *what* actual figures to feed into them. As we have said before we have no answer to this problem other than to muster all the accuracy that one possibly can; to give careful consideration to the probabilities involved; not to disregard the value of reliable records about past performance on the farm in question, and to make the most careful estimate possible of likely prices and costs for the time period in question; all easier said than done. Clearly, to project too far foward is to trespass on the unknown. It is our belief, however, that farmers themselves are usually best placed to prepare their own budgets; and if an outsider is employed 'to hold their hand' it is still likely that the best place to prepare the budget is on the farm in question, along with the farmer, and with all the available data, not in an adviser's or consultant's office miles away.

The layout and calculations required for a complete budget are shown below and it is hard to envisage the circumstances in which it is wise to farm without a budget of this kind as a routine management tool.

Inputs

Purchased feed:
  productive units ×
  quantity per unit ×
  cost per unit

Purchased seed:
  as for feed

Fertiliser:
  as for feed

Rent and rates:
  actual level, allowing
  for possible increase

Power & machinery:
  previous figures,
  appropriately adjusted,
  or separate estimates
  for each item involved

Labour:
  calculate person by
  person, allowing for
  increases, plus casual, etc.

Other costs:
  previous figures,
  appropriately adjusted,
  or separate estimates

TOTAL

Outputs

Crops
  productive units × yield
  per unit × market price

Milk
  as for crops

Cattle ⎫
       ⎬ Productive Units × yield per
Sheep ⎪ unit × market price (or, if
       ⎬ more appropriate, value
       ⎪ increase). Allow for
       ⎬ replacement stock by
Pigs   ⎪ specifying sales (eg. culls
       ⎬ and surplus young stock)
       ⎪ and purchases, if
Poultry⎭ replacements not home reared.

Sundries
  itemise and value

TOTAL

PARTIAL BUDGETS

This is the financial management tool that farmers and managers are likely to require more than any other. The reason for that is simple. It is a method of assessing what any alert manager will be constantly turning over in his mind; the possibility of advantageous change. Expansion, contraction, the introduction or discarding of activities, or a change in methods of production, can all be examined with the help of the partial budget. It embraces only those items of cost and return that will alter as a consequent of the contemplated change. When farmers talk of 'back of the envelope' calculations it is the partial budget approach that they are really talking of. Formally it takes the following form and answers the vital question, 'Is the total gain greater than the total loss?'.

Gain	*Loss*
Extra revenue?	Lost revenue?
Avoided costs?	Extra costs?
Total	Total

The great value of this tool suggests that more should be written about it; in fact, its simplicity leaves relatively little to be added. It should be emphasised, however, that it cuts right across the concept of fixed and variable costs, taking account of *any items* that in any particular situation, will change. In some very simple situations, where for instance, two enterprises are being compared and where no change in fixed costs is envisaged a comparison of the gross margins, at whatever scale of change is involved, will in effect constitute the partial budget. More often than not, however, an orthodox partial budget will be required and will be safer.

The methods of calculating individual items of input and output are similar to those used for complete budgeting. The one difficulty that exists in partial budgeting which is not present in complete budgeting is, literally, that of identifying the items that will change. In complete budgeting, everything, by definition, is included. In some respects, therefore, partial budgets need more careful thinking about. But as in all things, practice makes perfect, and all farm managers should certainly cultivate this particular practice.

BREAK EVEN BUDGETS

This kind of budget can be useful where there is some doubt about the level of any particular variable, and the effect of possible variations in that level needs to be examined. This may be the case, especially, when a new enterprise is involved and there is nothing in the farm records to go on. The technique can be applied to either complete or partial budgeting situations. Important elements of yield or price can be varied to show the financial effect of different eventualities and, in particular, the minimum level of performance required to cover known costs. To take a very simple example, if on an all arable farm, total costs were known to be £x per hectare, and the expected price of cereals is £y per tonne, then the break even yield will be x/y tonnes per hectare.

The technique could equally well be applied to inputs, but is more usually associated with outputs. It is very much a trial and error approach, with one variable under the microscope at a time. In reality, of course, numerous variables will be influencing results at the same time. There may be a need, therefore, for a series of different budgets to test the effect of a whole range of possible price and yield levels in critical enterprises. This approach is known as sensitivity analysis – a practice that has much to commend it in times of uncertainty. At all events there is a case for more than one budget: a conservative one, assuming the worst; a target one, aiming at the best; and for control purposes, a best possible estimate of what might actually happen. There is much to be learned from budgetary explorations of this kind. If a trading account answers the question, 'what *has* been done?', it is budgeting, in its various forms, that answers the more important forward looking questions: 'what *has* to be done?', 'what *should* be done?' and 'what *might* be done?'.

CASH FLOWS

A rather different kind of budget is the cash flow. It is not new to farming but it has been given new prominence in recent years as inflation and increased uncertainty of prices and costs have given rise to new liquidity problems. A cash flow is merely a method of setting out *actual* cash outgoings and incomings over a period of time, indicating when each transaction is expected to occur, and what effect this will have, at any point of time, on the cumulative balance: the bank balance or overdraft. A bank statement is, in fact, a kind of cash flow presented after the event.

The flow can be drawn up to suit the requirement of the individual or organisation concerned. It can relate to trading items only (although its purpose would then be very limited) or include also capital and personal expenditure, which is more usual. It can stretch as far ahead as is required (although after a couple of years it becomes increasingly speculative) and information can be set out in any required units of time, e.g. monthly, quarterly or annually. The balance can be struck for each time period, and a cumulative balance (beginning with the balance – overdraft existing at the commencement of the calculations) carried forward

The framework for a cash flow looks like this:

Item	← Time periods →			
receipts itemised →				
sub total (1)				
expenses itemised →				
sub total (2)				
balance for each time period (1) – (2)				
cumulative balance				

Over the years this kind of statement has been called a capital diary and a capital profile but has more recently been referred to as a cash flow.

It has a variety of uses, as follows:

(a) For discounting future returns from investment projects.
(b) For assessing the feasibility of investment projects, or simply, the continuation of existing operations.
(c) For knowing and being able to tell a lender, the expected future level of a bank balance–overdraft.
(d) For simply forecasting the future pattern of events (i.e. the use of inputs, the receipt of outputs, the incidence of personal spending, including tax payment, and of planned investments, etc.)
(e) As a means of adjusting the timing of payments and sales to the advantage of the business.
(f) As a control check against which events can be monitored as they happen.

In (a) and (b) the entries would be limited to items related to the projects in question.

In the United Kingdom numerous advisory and commercial organisations, using computer facilities, offer cash flow and related services to the farming community. They are a valuable aid to management simply in charting the way forward. Bricks cannot be made without straw, however, and meaningful cash flow projections cannot be drawn up without first some orthodox annual budgets of the type already discussed in this chapter. The allocating forward of receipts and expenditure must be based on some assessment of what the total for the time period in question will be. Unlike the annual budget, however, the cash flow will depict a distinct shape, with peaks and troughs, which will reflect the nature of the farming system in question as well as something perhaps of the attitudes and trading habits of the individual farmer concerned.

Before leaving the subject of budgeting behind – and moving on to Balance Sheets – there is a final word to be said. Most discussion and writing about budgeting makes the basic assumption that, difficult as it may be, it is nevertheless possible to quantify all of the items involved. In fact, this is not the case, especially where fairly major investment projects are involved – as opposed to minor adjustments to existing systems – when some of the benefits that are being sought are in the form of improved technical performance and/or reduced physical and mental strain for operators and managers. A good example would be the introduction of a rotary parlour. Certain benefits of the kind just suggested will be hoped for but cannot be guaranteed, and even if they do in fact occur, it may be impossible to actually measure them. This problem is akin to those encountered on a much larger scale in major public investment projects, where recourse is made to cost-benefit methods. We would not suggest that farmers become involved in that kind of exercise but the fact remains that decisions which sometimes involve intangible items do have to be made. Despite the difficulties, systematic thinking is still likely to help. It will, therefore, always be sensible to proceed *as far as possible* with the appropriate budgets. If all of the credit items cannot be quantified at least a net cost can usually be arrived at against which hoped for benefits can be weighed in the mind. Judgements of this kind will be very much better than nothing, if they only serve to identify where, approximately, the break even situation lies.

BALANCE SHEETS

STRUCTURE AND MEANING OF A BALANCE SHEET

If a trading account has some of the characteristics of a film, showing what is happening through time, then a balance sheet can be more likened to a snap shot. It describes the financial state of a firm at a particular point of time. The trading account is more concerned with performance; the balance sheet with status. In principle, it is a straightforward enough document to understand, although in practice, the variations in layout and terminology that are employed by different accountants often create confusion. This no doubt has something to do with the fact that some farmers we have known have found considerable difficulties in interpreting their balance sheet; sometimes referring jointly to their trading accounts and balance sheets as 'the accounts', without clearly differentiating between the two.

We believe that it helps to have a simplified view of what to look for. Basically, all balance sheets show the total *assets* employed in a firm, and balance them against the *liabilities*.

These two sets of information are usually set out side by side (but are sometimes presented in vertical form) and will look like this:

Liabilities	Assets
Current	Current
Longer term	Fixed
Net worth _____	_____
_____	_____

In this sense, asset simply means the capital employed whether it is very liquid (like cash in hand) or very fixed (like land). The balance sheet convention is normally to list assets in ascending order of liquidity, with cash at the top and land at the bottom. It is usually subdivided into the current assets, at the top, including such items as cash in hand, bank balances, debts owed to the business, stores on hand and trading livestock, followed by fixed assets including breeding livestock, machinery and equipment, land and buildings. In many ways this is a rather arbitrary division of things, but it conveniently describes the situation.

Since, in an accounting sense, businesses are deemed to have an existence of their own, all of these assets must have been financed by somebody and ultimately – should the business for any reason be wound up – owners of capital will want it returned. To the extent that the proprietor himself is an owner of some of this capital, he takes his place amongst the others to whom the business has a liability. This allows all of the assets to be balanced equally against all of the liabilities. The assets describe how the capital is deployed; the liabilities describe who owns it. Like the assets, the liabilities are conventionally arranged in ascending order of liquidity and are also divided into the current and the longer term items. The former consists of such items as any debts owing by the farm, overdraft, tax debts, etc., and the latter of longer term private loans and fixed term loans such as mortgages. Hopefully, assets will exceed the liabilities to outsiders, and the proprietor will then own the balance. This amount is known as the net worth. It is the owner's stake in his own business, and is also known as the equity capital. If it is positive, the firm is solvent, which means that if it sold out, realising all of its capital, all liabilities could be met, with something left over. If liabilities to others outmatch the assets, the reverse would be true, with all that that implies.

That, quite simply, is the essence of the balance sheet. Any balance sheet (no matter how complicated its detail looks) should be read with that simple conceptual framework in mind. Any more complicated view of it is probably unhelpful.

BALANCE SHEET RATIOS

In recent years, in the United Kingdom at least, it has been fashionable to look for ways in which balance sheet ratios may be calculated and used. It is undoubtedly true that like the trading account, the balance sheet has messages to offer. Certainly, managers should be able to recognize and interpret the appropriate messages, but to calculate too many apparently precise measures and base decisions too closely on them is probably mistaken. Pressure to become involved in this area of management may have been placed upon the farming community by the ancillary and consultancy brigades. Fortunately, there is a healthy safeguard in that most farmers learn to become good judges of what is useful to them – and what is not – and not only in this area of management. We have yet to meet the farmer who indulges in sophisticated balance sheet calculations, although no doubt there are some who do and who get some benefit from them. Quite the best guide to this subject that we know is the article, listed in Further Reading, by Ian Reid. He discusses the meaning of the *messages* rather than the *arithmetic*. Important amongst these messages are: the need for a healthy net worth (many bankers like to see an owner having about a 50% stake in his own business); the riskiness of a 'high gearing' situation in which net worth is allowed to be too low and high borrowing charges have a first and heavy call on profits; the need to maintain a healthy balance between current assets and current liabilities so that any call to repay short term borrowing (including overdrafts) can be met without recourse to disposing of non-liquid assets – a situation known as 'overtrading'; the importance of flexibility that comes from a healthy degree of liquidity; and, finally, the importance of maintaining a sensible balance between current and fixed assets. Too much capital in fixed assets without the working capital to farm them, will produce a sterile situation.

Reid uses the analogy of an over-bodied car that will be easily overtaken by its competitors on the road. His article deserves reading.

Apart from the matter of return on capital – which we turn to next – we doubt if there is more that most farmers–managers need to extract from their balance sheets nor even, perhaps, whether they actually need to calculate ratios as such. An ability to recognise, and balance in the mind, the various absolute amounts that have been discussed here, will tell a lot. Some of the ratios, in fact, will become self evident from that inspection. We would conclude that it is certainly important for a manager to have a good understanding of balance sheet layout, to appreciate a limited number of relationships within it, and to be able to recognise trends over time. A great deal in all this will depend, however, on the competence of the individual, on how others see him, and on his own attitudes to risk.

RETURN ON EXISTING CAPITAL

Since the balance sheet tells us how much and what kind of capital is invested in a business, it is natural that we have to look to it when we wish to relate the profit, as depicted in the trading account, to the amount of capital that was required to generate it. In doing so, however, two important points must be remembered. First, that a balance sheet is struck once a year and therefore represents a measure of the capital employed only at that point of time. A more accurate measure would need to take account of the fluctuations, particularly in working capital, employed throughout the year. That can be done with the help of cash flow calculations, but it is time consuming and research work into this area has indicated that the errors involved in taking simple year end figures are not great. Secondly, the asset figures in any balance sheet are as accurate as the valuations employed. If, as is often the case with long term assets, they have remained unadjusted while asset values have in fact increased, they will clearly be inaccurate. The true capital actually invested in a business at any point of time is the capital that could be taken out at that same point of time and reinvested elsewhere.

The thought of doing just that may be one of several reasons why a farmer wishes to calculate the current return on his capital.

He may also wish to compare himself with the 'going rate' for his type of business or with the returns he achieved in his own business in previous years. Several different kinds of calculations can be made depending on the ownership circumstances and questions to be answered. Three of them will be mentioned here.

First, there is *return on the tenant-type capital*, reflecting the result of farming the land as opposed to owning it. It is calculated as follows:

$$\frac{\text{Profit (management and investment income)} \times 100}{\text{All capital except land and buildings}}$$

(The management and investment income is the residual after a charge has been made for unpaid manual labour)

The magnitude of this figure will clearly vary according to the potential of the farming system involved and the capability of the individual. In recent years, in the United Kingdom, the figure for many orthodox farming systems has on average ranged between 15% and 20%. It should be remembered, however, that the profit figure used here conventionally includes a return to management as well as to capital.

Secondly, of more interest to the owner occupier, there is return on all the assets employed, including the land, i.e.:

$$\frac{\text{Profit (without any charge for rent)} \times 100}{\text{All capital (tenant's and landlord's)}}$$

The average level of this calculation is inherently much lower than that for tenant-type capital, and is frequently down in the low single figures.

A third and important measure, that will be of interest to any farmer (tenant or owner occupier) who includes borrowed money amongst his liabilities, is the net return, after borrowing charges, accruing to his own share of the capital. This time the calculation will be:

$$\frac{\text{Profit less interest on borrowed capital} \times 100}{\text{Total capital employed less borrowed capital}}$$

All of the three measures described here have two things in common. First, caution should be exercised in placing too much reliance on the absolute accuracy of any such calculation. Warnings have already been sounded about the inexactitude of profit calculations and of asset valuation. It should be remembered, therefore, that calculations of return on capital may compound any errors. Secondly, these rates of return are concerned with past results and, by themselves offer no insight into the performance levels that have brought those results about. Historically they are of interest and may satisfy certain curiosities, but they have a limited value when it comes to directing the future deployment of capital. That is, in many ways, a more interesting and important topic and is the subject of the fourth and final section of this chapter.

INVESTMENT APPRAISAL

THE IMPORTANCE OF FRESH INVESTMENT

Many farmers complain that in recent years they have had to 'pedal' faster and faster in order to stay where they are. Translated into financial terms they are saying that they have had to itensify and to invest more and more in order to maintain existing profit margins. It is hardly surprising, therefore, that we have seen an increasing awareness in farming circles of capital problems – of how to get hold of it and how to use it – and that investment appraisal as a subject has tended to feature more strongly in farm management literature, just as comparative analysis, budgeting and, finally, gross margins did during the fifties and early sixties.

To the extent, however, that existing investment represents a past commitment and is very often irrevocable, the element of agricultural capital that should come under the closest scrutiny is that small share of it that is being freshly invested and remains uncommitted until it has actually been invested. In theory, even past investment is constantly being freshly invested in the sense that if it is decided to leave it where it is, it is, in effect, being 'reinvested' in its present use. Also, some farmers do make positive provisions for reinvestment, occasionally making major alterations to their farming systems, and, therefore, to their patterns of investment. By far the greater proportion of farm capital, however, tends to remain more or less where it is and good management in the general sense of the word provides the best assurance that an adequate return accrues to it.

APPRAISAL METHODS

This situation makes it all the more important that whenever an opportunity presents itself to make a considered decision about whether or not to invest in a particular way, the opportunity should not be neglected. In practice, farmers and farm managers confront this opportunity in a variety of ways. In our experience, it is only occasionally that formal investment appraisal techniques are applied. Despite the recent interest in these techniques it remains a fact that the more sophisticated of them (e.g. discounted yield and net present value methods) are very infrequently used, and even the more simple methods – 'pay-back' and 'return on outlay' – only occasionally so. This is a pity. Application of the last two appraisal methods referred to is not complicated and even if applied in a rough and ready way would add some degree of worthwhile objectivity to the more intuitive approach. The return on outlay method simply relates additional profit expected from an investment, calculated as in a partial budget, to the extra capital required, i.e.:

$$\frac{\text{Extra profit} \times 100}{\text{Extra capital}}$$

Admittedly the extra capital may not be as easy to calculate in net terms as the extra profit, especially where there is an offsetting effect on the *new* capital required from *old* capital that might be released. Sometimes it is suggested that the return should be calculated on half of the new investment on the assumption that, because of depreciation, any investment will vary from its initial value to zero. This, however, overlooks the fact that the initial amount has to be found and that, in theory at least, a depreciation fund should be used to keep this investment intact.

The pay-back method of assessment simply involves dividing expected profit (before any charge for depreciation has been made) into the investment required, and measures how many years it will take to recoup that investment, i.e.:

$$\frac{\text{Total extra investment}}{\text{Extra annual profit}}$$

This method provides an appraisal expressed in time, compared with the percentage answer provided by the return on outlay method. Both assessments are fairly crude compared with those methods based on discounting – the discounted yield and the net present value – which have considerable advantages when major projects are involved, which are expected to yield a return over an extended time period and with unequal returns as between the years. Both of these techniques take account of the fact that because of the interest earning capacity of capital, funds returned today are worth more than a similar quantity returned tomorrow. To take account of this fact, discounting tables or formulae (the opposite of compounding) can be applied to future returns in order to equate them with present day values. This, in essence, is the logic of this kind of investment appraisal technique. They nevertheless remain vulnerable, like any budgetary techniques, to attempts to project anticipated costs and returns too far ahead. As we have already said, such methods, though not as complicated as they sometimes appear, are not often used by farmers and seem to us unlikely to be so. Any farmer or manager, however, who is anxious to acquaint himself with the arithmetic of this approach should consult the relevant chapters in either Sturrock's or Norman and Coote's book. Otherwise, if it is intended to use these techniques, specialist help will almost certainly be required from an experienced adviser.

More often than not, however, investors are inclined to follow a particular line because instinctively they believe it to be right or simply because they want to do it. These largely intuitive reasons for investing can be perfectly sound ones, especially if they are influenced by past investment which (with a due regard for future possible price and cost trends) has proved to be sound. By themselves, however, it cannot be denied that these intuitive approaches do lack the objectivity of some more formal investment appraisal and must always be suspect for this reason. So long as this state of affairs continues to exist, some more systematic but palatable kind of appraisal could help to provide a safeguard against the inadvertent misuse of capital. With this thought in mind we offer, the following *checklist* as a kind of investor's safety net, and we address our questions directly to the reader who may be thinking about new investment.

INVESTMENT CHECKLIST

(1) First, and foremost, have you looked for ways of improving income without using extra capital at all? There may be – indeed usually are – opportunities for tightening up on management or adjusting existing systems of farming which may even release capital. These opportunities should be fully explored before more capital is pumped in. In the majority of cases, and if properly interpreted, the established methods of farm business analysis (of the kind discussed earlier in this chapter) will provide an adequate guide here. If, however, fresh investment really is required, or you are simply seeking an outlet for spare cash, then:

(2) Have you budgeted for the change? This should *always* be done, using a partial budget. Weigh the extra returns and avoided costs against the extra costs and lost returns. If possible relate the answer to the extra capital involved. Ignore things that will not change.

(3) Are you giving priority to those enterprises from which you can be reasonably certain of a measurable return? Or are you just hoping, in some vague way, that things will be better?

(4) Are you about to expand a job that you know you are doing well? This usually means knowing the gross margins for your various enterprises. And what about the relative future prospects for each of them?

(5) If you are about to commit yourself to a new venture, have you made sure that you have the true facts about it? Or have you relied on hearsay or vague reporting?

(6) How long will you have to wait for your return? Investment always means outlay now for a return some time in the future. The further ahead that future is, the more uncertain any forecast of the return will be. Other things being equal, a return sooner is preferable to a return later.

(7) If necessary, can your investment be liquidated and reinvested in another form? A certain amount of investment in fixed equipment will always be necessary, but the ability to transfer capital from one enterprise to another may be a valuable tactic, especially for the younger farmer, who usually needs capital but often finds it hard to borrow.

(8) Will the new investment actually generate income? Livestock and crops, by their very nature, do this. Other types of investment (e.g. buildings, roads, machinery), necessary as they may be, merely assist. By themselves they generate nothing except costs. A reasonable balance between the two types of capital must be maintained, but always with sufficient of the income-generating kind.

(9) Are you carrying out your investment in the cheapest possible way, consistent with your own technical standards? There are two aspects of cheapness: the interest you will pay on borrowed capital, and the amount of capital that is actually employed. It is easy to pay too much attention to the former and not enough to the latter. The question to ask is, 'how little capital do I need?' not, 'how much?'. A well conceived and presented plan in these terms will help to convince a lender that you have a good case.

(10) Finally, if you are investing on labour saving grounds, where is the saving? Is your wages bill actually being reduced, or is there to be some additional output as a result of labour being released? Sometimes, especially where competition for labour is strong, it may be necessary to invest simply in order to keep the labour you have. But where so-called labour saving is the motive, be quite clear in your own mind about what this really means to the farm economy.

It seems appropriate to conclude this chapter by repeating an earlier thought, namely that the use of capital is what farming is all about. Many investment decisions centre around the word 'choice'. The choice between different investment possibilities on many farms is endless, as is the range in the returns that these investments can offer. Well conceived, marginal investments on existing and well managed farms can provide very good returns indeed; ill conceived, the return can be nil. Where no formal appraisal of an investment is being undertaken – and, as previously suggested, this is often the case – the use of a checklist of the sort offered here may help to provide some added assurance that investments are well conceived rather than ill conceived. Next time you are contemplating fresh investment have a good look at this checklist, especially question one.

SOME QUESTIONS RELATING TO THIS CHAPTER

(1) Why are most farm trading accounts an inadequate tool, in their raw state, to assess performance within individual enterprises? What kind of procedures are necessary to make them useful in this respect?
(2) Would some form of enterprise account, going beyond gross margins, be of value to you?
(3) Do you prepare a complete budget for your farm each year? If so, what use do you make of it? If not, why not?
(4) If your business was wound up, what proportion of its capital would you be left with? What is this called? Has it altered during the last three years?
(5) What is the essential difference between return on existing capital and return on fresh injections of capital? Why is the latter so important?
(6) What procedures do you adopt and what factors do you take into account when contemplating new investment?
(7) What improvements might be made to your farm without recourse to any new capital?

A GUIDE TO SELECTED FURTHER READING

Sturrock, F. G. 1971. *Farm Accounting & Management*. London: Pitman.
  The best book that we know on accounting and book-keeping aspects of farm management.
Norman, L. and R. B. Coote 1971. *The Farm Business*. London: Longman.
  Chapter 5 contains helpful examples of the arithmetic of investment appraisal.
Reid, I. G. 1969. Balance Sheet Interpretation. *Farm Management* 1, no.6, 8-14.
  Still the best and most readable assessment of the subject that we know.
Crozier, J. R. *Counting the Cash and the Capital*. Planning is Profitable: Number Two. Billingham: ICI.
Williams, A. J. *The Farmer as a Financial Manager*. Planning is Profitable: Number Four. Billingham: ICI.
  These two ICI publications provide useful 'popular' accounts of the subject.
Davies G. D. D. and W. J. Dunford, *Analysing the Financial Stability of the Farm*. Farm Economic Notes, No.25, 1979. Agricultural Economics Unit, University of Exeter.
  A very helpful, brief, and easy to read guide, including a worksheet to take the reader through the relevant stages of analysis; also contains other useful references.

10
Staff

Positive and negative contributions to efficient staffing

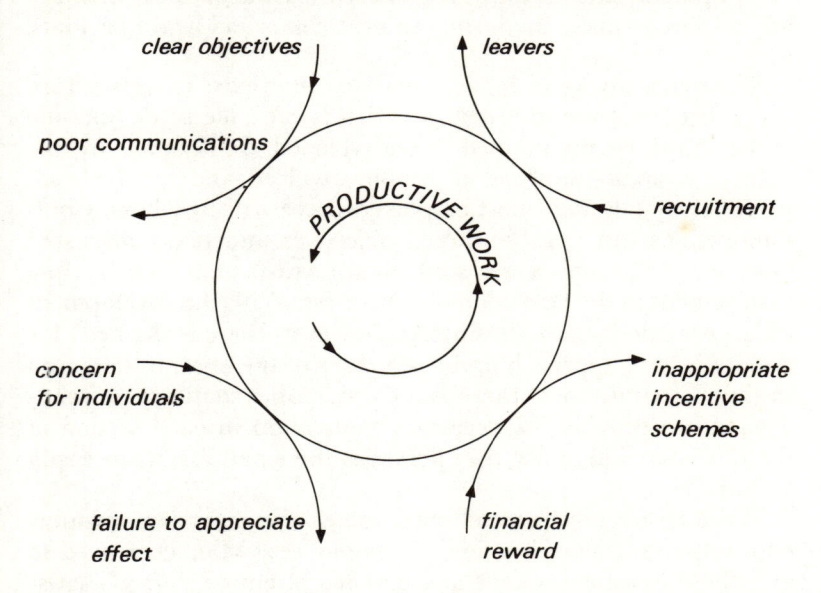

- clear objectives
- leavers
- poor communications
- recruitment
- concern for individuals
- inappropriate incentive schemes
- failure to appreciate effect
- financial reward

(PRODUCTIVE WORK)

This is yet another important chapter. It concerns the farm staff which is the resource which holds the key to productivity. Farm labour is important as a *quantitative* element in the cost of production, but more so as a *qualitative* influence on the efficient use of all other resources.

A notable feature of the farming industry in many countries, but especially in the UK, has been the continued reduction in the size of the work force, increased mechanisation and a corresponding increase in labour productivity. Heavy manual chores remain as a feature of the work on some smaller farms but the tendency is to expect the majority of workers to be equipped with a wider range and higher level of skills. There is an enormous range in the working conditions from one holding to another, but on the whole, farm work offers both interest and satisfaction. The work, except in certain types of intensive enterprise, is varied by season, by day and even within the hour. Of considerable significance is the fact that at the completion of a work period, staff can usually see clearly what has been achieved. It may well be a field cleared of bales or a group of animals vaccinated – in this case seeing the empty bottles. Some jobs can be so repetitive as to be monotonous and others unpleasant and dirty, but the increasing availability of equipment, such as improved safety cabs and air-flow helmets, are helping to make the farm a safer, cleaner and healthier place to work.

The generally good labour relations that exist in agriculture are a feature of the industry in which it can take pride and one which must be maintained and developed. It is aided by the relatively small numbers of people involved and by the close personal contact that most employees have with the boss. Communications can then be direct, objectives and plans discussed and agreed. In most cases staff obtain satisfaction from a close involvement in the operation of a business. With the development of larger scale farming businesses, however, there is the need for a more formal approach to the structure of the organisation, and in these circumstances there is a considerable challenge to management to provide the necessary motivation in each section of the business. The unity that pervades the small farm can easily be lost.

Wage levels, housing and other material factors are undoubtedly important considerations to employees. Managers need to give these items every care and detailed attention, but job satisfaction is also a factor which has the most marked effect upon labour productivity. We now go on in this chapter to examine the various aspects of this part of management that managers need to consider in order to create the optimum environment, and we begin with the important topic of staff planning.

STAFF PLANNING

It is possible that many farms operate, at any given point of time, with the labour force which they happen to have acquired over a period and that factors other than a genuine present need, in the economic sense, will have influenced this situation. The supply of labour, therefore, may or may not match the real present need of the farm. An objective and continuing assessment of the labour requirements and availability should therefore be made both for the present and with a watchful eye on the future.

Techniques of varying sophistication are available for use in staff planning according to the scale of the business, but in all situations the thought processes should be the same. The essence of staff planning is that after overall objectives have been established, a clear endeavour is made:

(a) to ensure optimum use of human resources currently employed, and
(b) to plan for future staff needs in terms of such aspects as skills, numbers, age and experience.

The planning process should result in the employment of the correct number of staff, having the necessary talents and skills doing the appropriate job, performing the right activities and above all working towards the achievement of objectives.

These ends are achieved by clearly defining objectives for the long and short terms, arranging activities to be carried out using the best methods and clearly defining the various jobs. Appropriate recruiting and training, as detailed below, can then take place to correct any weaknesses in the existing staff.

Assessing the number of workers required to run a farm can be done, especially for small enterprises, without too much fuss by experienced judgements. However, in the more complex situation, where some calculation is required, it is best done by using the 'standard man days' approach. This is a rather simple technique and is by no means perfect. It involves multiplying the hectares of each crop and the headage of each different livestock type by a known 'standard man day' figure (i.e. 8 hours). It is usual to add 15% to the total to allow for maintenance work and the results need to be interpreted in the light of such factors as the type and layout of livestock buildings, the availability and capacity of machinery, soil type, and, especially, seasonal variation of labour requirement with crops. A labour profile can be prepared to illustrate seasonal peaks and troughs. It should not be interpreted too literally but used as a guide to indicate problem periods. Consideration can be given to minimising peak requirements by improved mechanisation, change of variety or modifications to the cropping programme. The use of casual labour and contract services can also be considered as can improvement of gang organisation. Peak requirements can often be dealt with in the smaller farm by inputs of family labour and in larger organisations by diverting staff who are at other times largely involved in maintenance duties. Having employees with a wide range of skills and a flexible attitude shown by their willingness to move from job to job is a considerable asset to any business.

RECRUITMENT

Having considered the need to match the skills and abilities of staff to the needs of the jobs to be done our thoughts can turn to recruitment. The opportunity to recruit a new member of staff is a most important occasion and one justifying considerable management input. On the average farm, it is an infrequent event, so that apart from being an opportunity to be used to the full, it follows that many managers get inadequate experience to become suitably skilled in this important function. Guidance can be obtained from published material including that which is listed at the end of this chapter, and recruitment is an essential part of the syllabus of training courses in staff management. It may well be advisable, in the case of a senior appointment or in the early years of a manager's career, to employ professional assistance.

The recruitment process can be divided into four parts:

(a) The job and the person required. Before commencing to replace a member of staff or to appoint an additional person, it is necessary to consider in detail and to decide if there is, in fact, a worthwhile vacancy. By increased mechanisation, and by re-organising duties, it may be that recruitment is unjustified. Some re-organisation may be essential if the person has left the farm because he or she found the job too difficult, too boring, or providing insufficient challenge. Knowing that there is a post to be filled, it is then of considerable value to the manager and to potential employees for details of the job to be written down, i.e. to prepare a job description. This will include essential aspects such as working hours, pay, holiday arrangements, housing, perquisites, as well as the responsibilities and associated authorities. It should also outline any particular difficulties and cover such items as the opportunities for training or development. It is a document that will be retained by the person appointed and a periodic check through the office copy is a worthwhile exercise for the employer.

After describing the job, a full description of the ideal person to fill the vacancy should follow. Applicants receiving such a document will be able to judge for themselves whether they wish to be considered further. The details will include age, family, health, experience, qualifications and skills. The level of intelligence, disposition and interests will be of importance, especially if the person is to take a post with responsibility or work in a team with existing staff. A suitable person may be available in the business but if not the next stage follows:

(b) Obtaining suitable candidates. For a proportion of vacancies, advertising in the local or national press will be unnecessary, but for others, and especially the most important jobs, the cost of advertising will be well justified. Some farmers, for instance, report better response by advertising for stockmen in the local papers of grassland areas of the West and North of Britain or for tractor drivers in the arable East. The advertisement needs to be attractive, clearly worded, without unnecessary detail, but with explicit application procedure. A well prepared application form is helpful in most instances although for manual type jobs, it can put off suitable potential applicants. The facility for such a person to make a reverse-charge phone call in the evening is probably more appropriate.

(c) Selection. A difficult task now follows in assessing the information received from applicants and in selecting the ones to be invited for interview. Being able to contact applicants by telephone is beneficial especially when making interview arrangements, but also for checking queries, finding out why they want to move, and at the same time gaining useful first impressions as to their general approach and personality. If it is possible, a visit to see the applicant in his present job, to meet his family and perhaps see how they care for the cottage is a very advantageous practice. The interview itself is a most important event requiring adequate preparation and should be used primarily to judge how well each candidate would be likely to fit the job, but also for them to decide, after full discussions, whether they would want the job. Time is usually a precious commodity when recruiting, as the person being replaced has probably already left the farm and the duties are being performed by other staff members or perhaps by the farmer himself. Nevertheless, interviews should not be rushed and time certainly allocated to showing applicants over the farm, the housing, location of shops, schools and introductions to other members of staff. Complications can arise in the timing of interviews in relation to vacation of the housing by the previous occupants. Ideally, candidates can bring their wives (or husbands) on the interview day and are able to obtain all the information they require to make a decision if they want the job. It is in the care and attention to such details of family arrangements that successful recruitment depends.

(d) Induction. Having checked on references and appointed the new member of staff, then a most important task follows in ensuring that an adequate induction into the job takes place. A good start is most beneficial but again it requires management time. Although the objectives of the business will have been explained at the interview, they will need to be clearly confirmed when starting employment. Standards of performance, husbandry methods, approach to tidiness and timekeeping all need to be confirmed. Providing a well labelled map of the farm together with lists of other essential information assists the settling-in process. As time progresses, performance will have to be checked against the agreed standards, training needs assessed and any difficulties that have arisen discussed in full. We, therefore, turn now to the question of training.

TRAINING

There is no doubt that with few exceptions, everyone involved in a farm business, and certainly the management, would benefit from an appropriate form of training. This should improve their performance either at once or in the future, helping the business either by increasing output, or by reducing costs, or by a combination of the two. Good training helps the individual to identify what he or she is trying to do, enables the job to be done more effectively which leads to additional pride, confidence and satisfaction. Attitudes towards training are important and managers need to demonstrate the above advantages, perhaps coupled with appropriate financial rewards. Older, skilled staff sometimes have difficulty in seeing any personal benefits from training and many new entrants to the industry fight shy of activities that look like an extension of school. Such employees will probably respond better initially to 'on-farm' training than by attendance at specialised centres.

On-farm courses are particularly appropriate to skills training so long as the instructor has the required ability for the job. Many farm workers who are themselves highly skilled operatives, either with machines or in livestock husbandry tasks, are uninterested or perhaps find difficulty in passing on their skills to the average trainee. On the other hand, a particularly bright and motivated trainee can learn much and improve his performance by working with such a person. A further benefit to on-farm training is the availability of resources to enable extended practice of the task in hand. 'Off-farm' training does tend to make better use of instructors' time and with the easier access to specialised aids, can in many situations be more effective. It is interesting to note in the United Kingdom, the development by the Agricultural Training Board of such sophisticated training aids as a model of a calving cow. A short period working with such an aid can provide wide experience (even if simulated) that would take years for a trainee to obtain in the work stituation.

As with learning to do anything, the most successful skills training programme involves regular practice on the farm with an amateur tutor supplemented by a number of short periods at a training centre, supervised by a professional instructor. In the United Kingdom, the formation of training groups, in recent years, is proving to be a useful method of on-farm training in that instructors are able to develop specialised knowledge of local situations and use their time in the best possible way.

Training at supervisory level does necessitate periods away

from the farm at a specialised centre with tutors implementing a carefully prepared syllabus, tailored to the needs of the group. Matching the needs of an individual to an appropriate course is of importance, as little is achieved from a course which is either above or below an individual's needs at that time. The fact that staff leave the everyday concerns of the farm for a short period and are in company with similarly situated people, often with identical problems, can in itself be rewarding to them. On return from supervisory level courses, staff should be encouraged to discuss their experiences, explain what they have learned and particularly what they consider can be, with value, applied to their job or to other aspects of the farm business. Training prior to future promotion is a wise move in organisations where such possibilities exist, but can lead to frustration if people consider that they are overtrained for the job they are doing.

We do not wish, however, to leave the impression that training is the prerogative of operatives. Top level managers have to identify their own weaknesses and also take steps to obtain appropriate corrective action by, for example, obtaining places on advanced farm management courses or on the more specialised courses related to specific management topics. Although the theoretical aspects of management can be covered in such courses and sophisticated aids such as video machines used to simulate practical situtations, the opportunities for on-farm practice of management skills are more difficult to obtain. Many top farmers and managers did, in the early part of their career, work under a successful farmer who not only showed them by example, but also took valuable time to explain the reasons behind his actions. Unfortunately such opportunities are rare, as successful managers tend to be busy managing and sometimes think that they have not the time to train the next generation.

Concluding our thoughts on this subject, it needs to be stressed that training should be an on-going process undertaken as and when appropriate. The introduction of new machinery or a technique to the farm would be such a time when not only do the operatives need detailed training but also the manager will need at least an 'awareness' session so that he is in the picture and can provide the management back-up which may be necessary at a later date.

MOTIVATION

We have stated earlier, that farm staff hold the key to productivity and now we need to consider the factors involved in motivating workers to give of their best. The human being is motivated by his basic needs. Firstly, the 'primitive' needs of food, shelter, safety and security. As his standard of living increases, the 'social' needs then become more relevant – the need to belong and the need to know that someone cares for his interests. The 'ego' need to feel important and to have a sense of achievement are important motivating factors.

Managers need to appreciate that they are dealing with individuals. Each individual will attach his or her own level of importance to such considerations as hours of work, rewards, amenities and even to job satisfaction. Team leaders, be they managers or foremen, need, therefore, to know each member of staff well enough to understand his or her attitudes and relationships with others. The skills and personalities of each individual need to be fitted into the overall plan for the farm so that each and everyone feels that he is a valuable member of an efficient team. Working conditions should allow people to take a pride in their work with their contribution being clearly recognised and fully appreciated and rewarded. The long standing gulf in the standard of living between the farmer and his staff, although narrowing, is still a reality in many situations. Despite this, farm workers show tremendous loyalty and are keen to defend *their* farm against such problems as vandals, poachers or other unwanted callers. Good team spirit is clearly demonstrated by a motivated staff at difficult or crisis times, such as a late harvest. Workers often give up their private commitments to work long hours for the good of the business.

To a proportion of workers, a ladder of opportunity is a motivating force. Such people need to be encouraged to obtain qualifications and take part in training courses. On the other hand, many farm workers are content in their situation and do not want to take additional responsibility.

A subject which cannot be ignored under the heading of motivation is that of incentive payments. We do not wish to go into the pros and cons of incentives in every farming situation but it is our view that they can, in general, cause more problems than they solve. It is notoriously difficult to arrange a scheme which is fair to both parties, which is easily understood, and which clearly reflects the efforts of the individual. So often in present day farming situations, hard work which was traditionally paid on piece-work rates has disappeared in favour of mechanisation, and decisions have to be taken by management which affect the performance of an enterprise as much as, if not more than, the efforts of the staff. Indirect payments such as profit-sharing schemes create similar problems and it is, of course, impractical to think about loss-sharing, especially in a difficult year when staff may have put in exceptional effort and yet profits remain low or non-existent. We repeat that we have expressed a personal view here. There is no right or wrong way to proceed. There are situations where incentive payments are made and seem to suit employer and employee alike. This is clearly a matter for each individual farmer and manager to consider and act on accordingly.

LEADERSHIP

From our experience in visiting a wide range of farms, it is very clear that there is a close correlation between good farmers and good leaders. Successful leaders have the ability to get the work done through their staff. They are good organisers, create team spirit, workers know clearly what has to be done and they get on and do it well. Delegation is not only practised but it is a major factor in their success. Although as we have said, there is so often a close working relationship between the farmer and his staff, this should not prevent employees showing respect for their leader. An efficient business can only operate where there is discipline, for example, in good timekeeping and where there is *one* leader. Communications are no doubt a key factor in leadership. Not only does a manager need to give clear instructions but he also needs to be able to *listen* to communications *from* staff. If, for example, there are any signs of discontent, this can then be dealt with quickly before it becomes a major issue.

As was mentioned in the chapter on Planning, it is important to involve staff in setting goals, as they are more likely to want to achieve them if they have been party to their preparation. Staff, where possible, should be allowed to control and monitor their own performance but that does not mean that managers do not need to supervise.

Staff need to be encouraged to work as a team and not as individuals. Some people find it difficult to ask for help but they should be encouraged to do so as, for example, when moving stock. Many hands not only make light work but also they make quick and effective work. A feeling of 'them' and 'us' can easily develop between staff working with stock and other outside staff. It is often the case that one group is not aware of the objectives of the other. This sort of problem can be minimised by arranging staff meetings but unless skillfully 'chaired' such occasions can be good opportunities for the more extrovert members of staff not just to have their say, but also to say it at some length. A better environment for obtaining the opinion of staff is to talk to each one privately, at least once each week, perhaps when handing over the wages. Such occasions can be used to enquire of the employee's family or any other items that the employer may be able to help with.

We do not pretend that leadership is a simple matter, and certainly, we do not offer any simple recipe. But neither do we think, in the normal way of things, that leaders are only born. Experience, training, the ability to put oneself in the other person's shoes and the ability to learn from one's own mistakes are all important ingredients in acquiring a leadership which, if properly used, will reflect itself throughout the business.

REDUCING STAFF NUMBERS

This chapter cannot be concluded without reference to the fact that sometimes employees leave an organisation. They do so when they are retiring, because they are moving to another job or because their employer wants them to leave. In all three situations problems can arise, but this is another function of management to be dealt with appropriately by planning, decision making and taking action.

Retirement can take place at the normal age when state pension becomes available, earlier for health reasons or be delayed in cases where the person can still cope with the job or if transferred to tasks which are less demanding. Discussions at an early stage not only allow management plans to be made, but also put the mind of the employee at rest. Housing accommodation can be a worry where a family has occupied a tied cottage which is required for replacement staff. Negotiations with local housing authorities well in advance of the expected date of retirement have in many cases helped to obtain rented property. The development of schemes to enable agricultural workers to buy their own houses while still occupying farm cottages would be of considerable benefit to the industry. Staff who have retired, usually like to keep in touch with the farm. They enjoy an opportunity to walk the farm or attend a harvest supper or other social occasion.

An employee moving to another job, can be doing so as part of his career development and so long as he has stayed sufficient time to make a worthwhile contribution to the farm and gives adequate notice, his moving should cause few difficulties. On the other hand, he may be leaving because the job has proved to be unsatisfactory and management will then have to take appropriate action as discussed under the section on recruitment.

The situation of a person leaving, because the employer wants it that way, can cause difficulties and be painful. It is difficult because (fortunately) it does not happen very often and because there are few guidelines on how to deal with the situation. The literature on personnel management is mainly concerned with finding and keeping staff rather than disengaging them. The occasion can be painful because strained relations are often involved and because individuals' private lives are affected.

Employees are asked to leave a farm for one or more of the following reasons:

(a) Redundancy. The choice is between implementing whatever change is necessary for economic reasons as soon as possible, or deferring the change until natural wastage takes place. Alternatively, staff may be transferred within the organisation, working hours reduced or surplus labour kept on to make life more tolerable or to permit future expansion. Managers have to find the most appropriate solution to their situation.
(b) Unsatisfactory Performance. Before contemplating disengagement, the employer needs to reassure himself that all has been done to match the skills and abilities of the man to the job to be done.

Appropriate training needs to have been considered as well as the possibility of a more suitable job in another enterprise. Beyond a certain point it may be unfair to keep a 'wrong' man, unfair to him, to other staff, to the employer and to the business. Management should then invite the employee to 'look around' and help in a genuine way to find the person a more suitable job. It is essential to observe any laid-down procedures in order to avoid accusations of unfair dismissal.

(c) Personal Incompatibility. Farms, like other organisations are generally the richer for having a wide variety of talents and dispositions. Employers have to put up with minor disagreements but positive action may be called for if prolonged personality difficulties upset staff motivations.

(d) Instant Dismissal. There are a very limited number of reasons, e.g. proven theft, which might justify instant dismissal. There are other occasions when for some particular reason the employer has had 'enough'. In such situations the presence of witnesses and proof of earlier warnings may be essential to keep within whatever the law requires.

Such problem cases may well be discussed with a representative of the staff union so that the outcome is seen to be fair to all concerned. The reasons for dismissal in such cases need also to be discussed with the rest of the farm staff.

The decision to end this chapter on the subject of staff dismissal may seem to be unduly pessimistic but we consider that it is a topic which had to be covered and this seemed to be the most appropriate location. The problems which are most likely to be encountered in respect of reducing staff numbers, however, will be minimised if the fullest attention is given to the issues which make up the remainder of the chapter.

SOME QUESTIONS RELATING TO THIS CHAPTER

(1) What aspects of staff management do you find most difficult?
(2) When did you last consider fully the training needs of your staff?
(3) Have you a member of staff due to retire in the near future, if so have you discussed with him/her all the implications?
(4) How could you improve communications in your business?

(5) Do you consider that you spend sufficient time inducting new members of staff?
(6) Are you aware of the major factors motivating the key members of your staff?
(7) What do you think characterises a good leader?

A GUIDE TO SELECTED FURTHER READING

Staff Management in Agriculture, 1977. MAFF Technical Management Note 22. Pinner, Middlesex: MAFF Publications.
A most useful guide to the principles of staff management.
Farm Management, 1971, **2**, no.1.
This issue contains a number of very readable articles on man management in agriculture and in other industries.
Barnard, C. S. and J. S. Nix 1973. *Farm Planning and Control*. Cambridge: Cambridge University Press.
Pages 132–42 describe in detail the appropriate techniques for use in planning farm labour requirements.

Part IV
THE MANAGER

11
Managing the manager

THE IMPORTANCE OF INFLUENCE

The style, effectiveness and outward image of any organisation is fashioned more by the influence of the person or persons in charge than by anything else. We all recognise this fact, without difficulty, in others and in other organisations: the shops that we buy in; the schools that our children go to; the garages to which we take our car. It is less easy to remember that it also applies to us. The principal aim of this chapter is to remind ourselves of that fact.

The effectiveness with which any farm 'ticks over' is, above all else, a reflection of the competence of its manager. The way in which employees go about their jobs, the extent to which crises do or do not occur, the extent, even, to which the weather seems allowed to interfere or not; all of these and many other aspects of a farm business reflect the way the manager manages, they reflect his 'management style'. Good planning, good decisions and good control pay dividends in the effectiveness of day-to-day operations; bad planning, bad decisions and bad control do the reverse.

All of that may seem very obvious and easy to agree with. The difficult part, for any of us, is remembering that it applies to *us* and then remembering to remember it. We suggest to the reader that it can help in this situation, if every manager reminds himself from time to time that he is part and parcel of his farm's resources; that he is not something apart from the other resources – not apart from the land, the capital and the staff whom he employs. In fact, he is a very important part of those resources, because of, not despite, the special role that he has. The fact that he organises, directs and controls the total, means that it is his influence that governs the effectiveness with which the combined bundle of resources is put to work. It is especially important, therefore, that he makes himself the most effective of them all; that he sees himself as a resource to be controlled along with all the others. The big difficulty is that he has to do it himself.

KNOWING ONESELF

An important part of getting the best out of others – of utilising their talents, giving reign to their ambitions, and promoting their job satisfaction – is to try to understand them, develop their strengths and not to aggravate their weaknesses. If this is true of our dealings with others, it is, no doubt, equally true of our dealings with ourselves. If we are to draw the best out of ourselves in the interests of the organisation that we manage, some understanding of our own capabilities and limitations, our aspirations and our fears, will be an essential part of the process. That was implicit in much of Chapter 3 when we discussed setting objectives and the task of matching available resources – including the manager – to realistic and obtainable objectives.

We do not see or offer any short cut in this process of acquiring self knowledge and, to some, it will come easier and quicker than to others. Formal education – both of a general and of a specialised nature – industrial training, experience in the job and, for many, some form of travel, service or experience quite outside farming, can each make a contribution to the full development of the individual. By this we mean having a maturity which facilitates both self understanding and a competence to undertake the management job in hand, including the employment and development of others. The paths that individuals tread in these matters, vary according to their circumstances and inclinations. We see no single path for an aspiring manager. We see, instead, varying degrees of education, training and experience of various kinds fusing together in different ways for different individuals; with one phase of life building on another, opening, informing and training the mind during its most receptive years.

The impact and influence of others on each of us will be of paramount importance in this process, and it will not be confined to the influence of those who teach us in a formal sense. It may well be, for instance, that the greatest single benefit to be derived for farm managers, if and when they attend training courses, will come more from the contacts they enjoy with fellow managers – each with his own set of problems – than from any tutor. And it could even be that training courses designed specifically to promote personal growth and development could be as valuable to a young farm manager, or to a farmer's son needing to assert his individuality, as any form of technical training.

THE INDIVIDUALITY OF FARM MANAGERS

Although each farm manager and farmer is an individual, unique to himself, there are good reasons to believe that they have many managerial problems in common. In a previous publication (Giles & Mills, see Further Reading) surveying the personal and professional characteristics of the men who are paid to manage British farms, one of the authors indeed, posed the question, 'Is there a typical farm manager?'. In reporting on the results of that survey, its authors pointed cautiously to certain, 'characteristics and attitudes which may perhaps typify many of the farm managers in this country'. They offered an *identikit* which included the following characteristics:

'... male; between 30 and 50 years of age; married; with a good secondary education and an agricultural qualification; four or five previous jobs; little or no experience outside the industry; in his first management post by the age of 30; operating on 'large' farms; satisfied with his work, but less satisfied with his terms of employment; and over half of them feeling seriously or slightly under-employed as managers.'

Notwithstanding this identikit, the authors concluded that:

'ultimately, of course, differences as well as similarities need to be taken into account – and this survey has certainly confirmed a wide range of circumstances among the respondents'

If that conclusion was valid for a small sample of salaried UK farm managers, who had joined the Farm Management Association, and who had bothered to reply to a questionnaire, how much more valid would it be for the managers who did not reply; for those who have not joined the Association, for those who are self-employed rather than salaried, or who manage farms elsewhere in the world?

In personal and agricultural terms the possible permutations in answer to that question could be endless. But in terms of the management problems associated with the job, we think that is much less likely to be the case. Earlier in this book, we have several times expressed the view that many of the management problems that face farming are very similar in essence to those facing other sectors of the economy. If that is true, then how can the strictly *management* problems encountered on one farm or another – or even in one country or another – differ greatly?

We see these problems as falling into two very broad categories. The distinction is a fine one, but, we think, valid. First, there are those problems that are primarily related to managing a farm, the technical, financial and organisational problems – and these have been discussed in the previous chapters. Secondly, there are those more personal problems that stem from being a farm manager, problems related to job satisfaction and personal development. The remainder of this chapter discusses some of them. It is based on a combination of research, observation and discussion with many of those involved.

THE PERSONAL PROBLEMS OF BEING A FARM MANAGER

(1) Farm managers are likely to be intellectually and professionally lonely. This problem results from the fact that farm managers are, usually, well educated, well informed people, but working in relative isolation. That implies no disrespect whatsoever to their staff, for whom we have the utmost respect. Nevertheless the farm manager (self employed or salaried) is relatively isolated – often *very* isolated – from his peers. Spontaneous consultations and discussion with equals – of the kind that those who work in larger organisations enjoy – are scarce. The individual may or may not feel that this is a disadvantage but some who are known personally to us certainly do, and try to make positive attempts to counteract the situation. This no doubt partly explains why farmers are such enthusiastic attenders at evening meetings, conferences, and farm walks. The industrial manager or professional man who has been with colleagues all day seems less eager for these things. Farmers and farm managers have a more genuine need in this respect. But they have to learn how to be discriminating in allocating their time in this way.

(2) Strange as it may seem farm managers can get bored. Occasionally, of course, we all can. It might be supposed,

however, that the job satisfaction associated with farming makes farmers and farm managers immune from this particular problem. This is not so, and they would not be human if it were. Indeed, the very slowness and in some cases the sameness of events, coupled with the isolation we have just discussed, can give rise to it. The likelihood of this happening depends on the individual and the size, nature, and complexity of the business concerned; but when it does occur, a careful blend of counterbalancing activities is needed. Getting off the farm, whether for social or professional reasons, can be an important antidote to boredom. So too can attending some form of training course. This should not be a prerogative of employees. Mixing with non-agricultural people can also help. Just filling in time is the worst possible solution.

(3) Closely related to the question of boredom is the fact that farm managers are often in danger of feeling under-employed in the strictly managerial sense. Do not mistake us. We are not saying that they are under-employed in total. The demands on their time and the scope for physical work, if nothing else, ensures that in most cases that is not so. Many farmers and managers have told us, however, that the amount of management input that is required – even on quite large farms, and especially if activities tend to be highly seasonal – does sometimes mean that they are not managerially fully extended. Different individuals cope with this problem in different ways. Some just accept it, and maybe allow Parkinson's Law to take over; others become physically involved in the operation of the farm and if there is no obvious alternative, they clearly provide a very convenient form of part-time labour with no opportunity cost; yet others look around for methods of intensifying their farming activities, in some cases to the extent, even, of managing a second farm; still others become involved in non-farming activities of different kinds, commercial, political or community service. A few, quite sensibly, enjoy recreation. This whole problem is clearly related to another one, that of organising managerial time – the next topic on our list.

(4) Farmers find it difficult to organise their own time. In this, they are often victims of their own circumstances. They

manage small businesses; they alone usually represent 'top management', and a wide variety of individuals – either the staff employed on the farm or members of the wide band of ancillary folk with whom farmers have to deal – will want access to 'the gaffer'. The sheer need to be available and to be ready to move from one job to another (often involving considerable travel), ensures that uncommitted time will usually be at a premium. The *ad hoc* nature of supervisory management takes over.

In these circumstances farmers can very easily become too busy doing the pressing things to have time for the important ones. Again, do not misunderstand us. There is a lot of time when the manager simply has to be available; it is a major part of his job. But it is equally important that there is time available – uninterrupted time – when he can do the important long term things. We do not subscribe to the view that a farm manager *has* to be available all the time any more than we would to the view that he *has* to be able to do every job on the farm. He has his own job to do, and more than anything else, it is to ensure that there continues to be a job for others. Drucker talks in The Effective Executive about 'discretionary time'; we talk about 'usable chunks of time'. Days or half days regularly set aside when the manager is *not available* to others; it is as if he was away. He has a pressing appointment – with himself. If a manager wishes to bring about this state of affairs he must do it for himself. No one else will help him. If the reader feels that this is required in his own case then he will need to look critically at how he uses his time and restructure it a little so that the necessary number of 'usable chunks of time' are made available. A degree of firmness will be required which will only be present if the individual concerned *wants* it to be. Farm staff will understand, if the matter is explained to them properly. Tell them that *you* are ensuring that *their* jobs will continue to be there, and recruit their assistance by delegating authority to them. They will respond to both of these things.

(5) Farmers, on the whole, are not good delegators. That is not surprising. In small businesses the scope for delegation – maybe even the need for it – might be slight. Many farmers, therefore, get little practice at the art, and practice, as in

all things, makes perfect. The word 'art' has been used here to describe delegation because that is what it is. It is not simply a matter of telling someone else to get on with a job that you do not want to do. Several steps are involved: first identifying the job and the responsibility involved; second, and very important, identifying the right individual to do it; third, instructing him and, also very important, giving him the appropriate authority to get on with it; and fourth, the most important of all, getting out of the way so that he can get on with it, in his own manner – leaving him alone but maintaining a correct degree of interest and support as and when required. It is not easy. But it *is* important to look for opportunities to delegate in a responsible way. It will help in the development of the careers and capability of others. It will also help to provide the freedom for the manager to undertake the various important tasks of management upon which the survival of a business may ultimately depend. Delegation can also help to remedy the vexed question, in farming, of long and often anti-social hours – to which we now turn.

(6) Farmers perhaps accept too readily long and irregular hours and short holidays. We have spoken to their wives as well as to them and know this to be true. It can have serious repercussions on family life. Sometimes, of course, it is inevitable and essential. Too often, however, we suspect that it is associated with 'living over the shop', with a mistaken feeling of indispensability and a reluctance or inability to delegate properly. But we know more than one farmer who lives in a town house and who literally, goes to work from nine to five.

(7) Farmers are not renowned for having regular recreational outlets. These are necessary in order to get away from their businesses and from farming, into a totally different and relaxing activity with fresh company. We cannot overestimate the importance of this; preferably an activity which involves a firm commitment, rather than one that you can choose to do if it is a pleasant day and you are not too busy when the time arrives. The rejuvenating effect of this kind of commitment – no matter what it is – will pay dividends when you return. You will see things in a better perspective; minor problems will be seen for what they are. Other

people, to whom you have delegated responsibility, will have managed in your absence. They will have enjoyed the responsibility vested in them and responded to it.

(8) Finally, there are various ways in which farmers and farm managers, like everyone else, can feel professionally insecure. This can arise from various reasons: from uncertainties stemming from a failure to have a clear idea of the immediate path ahead, either because the individual concerned has found it difficult to identify his objectives and his subsequent plans, or because, in the case of the salaried manager, his employer has not encouraged this approach. Insecurity can also arise from a lack of professional confidence. This is closely associated with the whole question of personal growth and will clearly affect some individuals more than others. It will usually lessen with advancing age. We believe, however, that more than a few farmers have a problem of this kind.

Managerially speaking, their circumstances are inclined to create a situation in which they can become jacks-of-all-trades and masters of none. They may not, for instance, talk with the authority of the banker, or the personnel manager, the sales manager or the production manager whom they meet in industry. This can and does sometimes create feelings of inferiority. It should not do so. The farmers' circumstances are entirely different from those of the specialists just referred to and it is our view that when compared with their true counterparts in the rest of the economy – general managers of other small businesses – farming's managers have no need to feel in any way inferior.

There is additionally, that other kind of insecurity that is sometimes the lot of the salaried manager. His employment is dependent upon the financial and family circumstances, and even the personal whims, of his employers. We have known some sad instances of this. Salaried managers are too small a group to exert much political influence on their own behalf, try as they might. We believe, however, that in the United Kingdom at least, the combination of legal safeguards against wrongful dismissal, the creation of provison against redundancy, and a growing awareness on the part of the employers of farm managers of the need for proper career opportunities through contracts of employment, promotion prospects and pension schemes, will all gradually improve the situation. But there is still a long way to go in this, even in this country.

CONCLUSION

This account of some of the personal problems that are likely to beset the manager of a farm may seem depressingly long and dismal in nature. It is not intended to be. We have not wished to imply that farmers or farm managers constitute an inadequate group of individuals incapable of dealing with the normal buffets that their occupation deals out. It is simply that, to a greater or a lesser extent, the problems that have been discussed here frequently do exist. Where they do exist, either individually or collectively, they can easily operate against the full development of the individual concerned. That in turn makes him a less effective manager than he might otherwise have been, and that in turn influences the effectiveness of the other people and resources employed in that business. Ultimately profits suffer.

In so far as we can, we have indicated or hinted at possible answers to these problems. There may, of course, not be precise answers in the sense that there are to various other kinds of problems. Whatever answers an individual finds, however, will reflect something of his own personality and of the environment in which he finds himself. Geographical differences between regions as well as between countries will have important influences. In almost all cases, however, answers to the kinds of problems and issues that have been discussed here will be *human* in character rather than *technical* or *financial*. Perhaps the most important factor where problems of this sort exist – and who would be brave enough in his own circumstances to suggest that none do – is that their existence should be recognised and openly discussed. That will go a long way towards providing an answer. The manager will then be on the way to managing himself.

SOME QUESTIONS RELATING TO THIS CHAPTER

(1) What aspect of managing your farm do you find most personally demanding? Why? What do you do about it?

(2) What specific steps do you take to avoid a situation in which you might feel professionally isolated?
(3) Are there times of the year, in particular, when your job bores you? If so, what do you do to counteract it?
(4) In what ways could you most easily enrich the managerial content of your working life?
(5) Do you delegate sufficiently and how do you go about it?
(6) How important do you think it is for you to be able to do every job on your farm and always to be contactable? Do you get regular relaxation off the farm?
(7) Are you satisfied that you have enough time to deal with the important long term aspects of your business? If you are not, what are you going to do about it? If you are, read this book again!

A GUIDE TO SELECTED FURTHER READING

Giles, A. K. and F. D. Mills 1970. *Farm Managers.* Miscellaneous Study no.47. Dept of Agricultural Economics and Management, University of Reading.
The results of a study commissioned by the UK's Farm Management Association.

Stewart, Rosemary 1970. *Managers and their jobs.* London: Pan Books.
A readable account of how 160 managers spend their time in industry.

Ansell, D. J. 1970. The Farmer and his time. *Farm Management* 1, no.8, 36–43.
An account of a mini Rosemary Stewart-type survey, conducted amongst farmers in Berkshire. Would assist anyone thinking of keeping his own timesheets.

12
Acquiring information

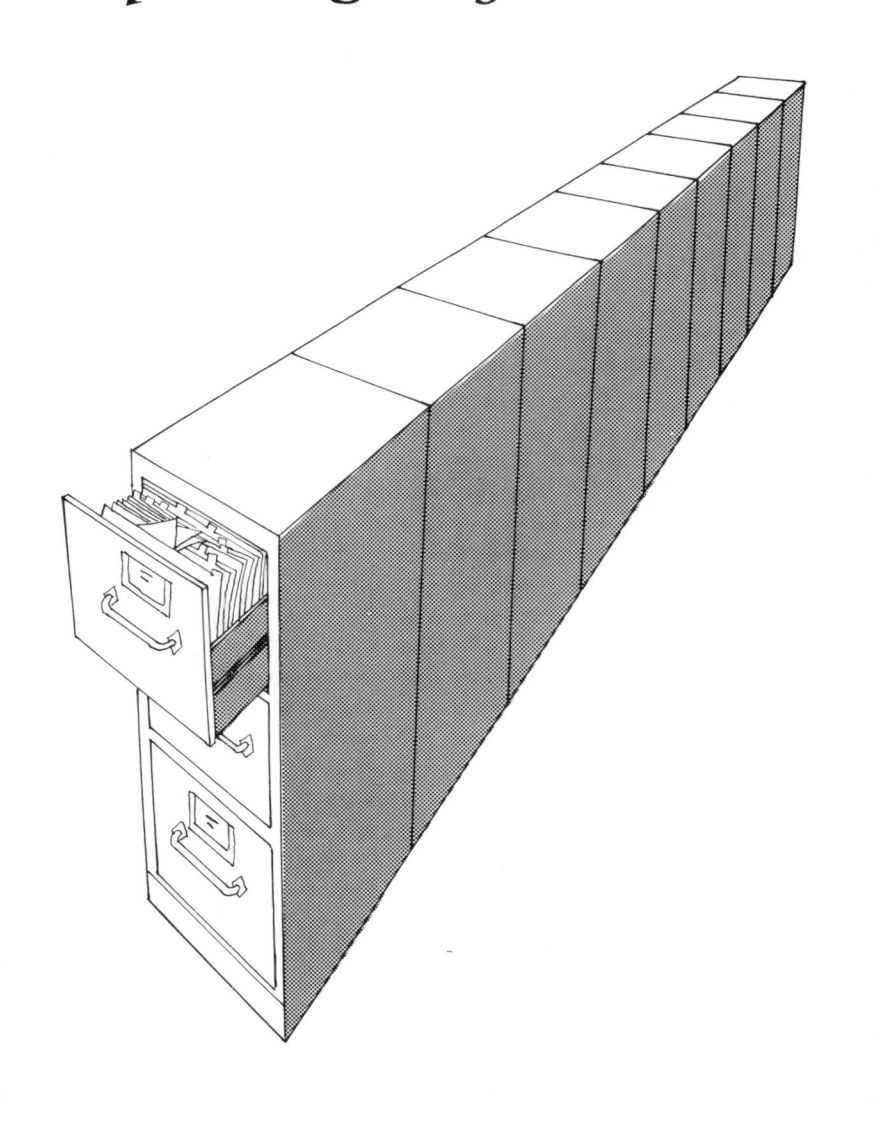

One aspect of management in which it is especially important for the manager to manage himself, is in the provision of information. Here, in particular, he needs to be well organised. We have, therefore, decided to devote a separate chapter to this subject and to place it in this final part of our book.

In the course of discussing various aspects of the management task, reference has been made to the importance of having the appropriate information. Indeed, it is the case that the four major management functions as outlined in Part II and the four areas of a business that have to be managed, outlined in Part III, are all, in some way or another, dependent upon the information that is available to a manager.

Thus, *setting objectives* for the business involves having a knowledge of the many factors which determine the environment in which the business has to operate. Managers need to involve themselves in a certain amount of reading, listening, and conversing with others so as to be aware of the economic and political constraints under which they have to manage their businesses.

The planning process involves using relevant physical and financial data obtained from both within and from outside the farm. Non-quantitative information is in many circumstances just as important as the quantitative. It may, for example, indicate that, once fully evaluated, one method of production eases the stress on management and workers compared with another.

Decision making clearly depends upon the availability of relevant information. It is an integral part of the task whether the decisions be of a strategic or tactical nature.

Control is similarly only possible when information is to hand. Control has to be 'against' something. Again this may be quantitative data in respect of inputs or outputs or it may include a wide range of other information, such as the cloddiness of a seedbed or the morale of staff, which will have a direct bearing on the control of day-to-day operations.

Management of the four areas of the business – production, finance, marketing, or staffing – also clearly necessitates having information that is appropriate to any particular matter in hand. We, therefore, now go on to consider in a little more detail the kinds of information to be acquired, their sources, and give some indication of how this information can be obtained and stored for future use.

KINDS OF INFORMATION

We have identified five main categories of information that a farmer requires – technical, financial, legal, international and environmental – and offer brief comment on each of these.

Technical

When considering production, it was clear that if farm enterprises are to be profitable they need, in the first instance, to be technically efficient. Prices of inputs and outputs are obviously very important, but we cannot stress too firmly that farmers are in the business of production in a technical way. New developments are continually available to the farmer, but he does need to obtain the necessary detailed information in order to be in a position to evaluate the likely benefit of such developments in his particular situation.

Take, for instance, the dairy farmer selecting a bull from the AI organisations, for use in breeding herd replacements. Published information is available relating to proven sires which indicate the improvements to be expected by the daughters of a bull over their contemporaries in terms of milk yield, quality and confirmation as well as such features as a tendency to produce heavy calves and associated calving difficulties. The bull may have a sufficiently high 'weighting' indicating that adequate daughters have been tested in a wide spread of herds to give the data adequate statistical significance. Nevertheless, wise dairymen also take opportunities to inspect as wide a selection of the daughters as possible and at the same time, where possible, to see the dams so as to be sure just how well the bull is correcting conformation faults. The prospective user may also want to discuss with the owner of the cattle, subjects such as temperament and slowness of milking. This kind of information is somewhat difficult to report in print. Visits to agricultural shows or to breeders farms to this end, take time, but they are of value, especially to herdsmen who will eventually have to milk and manage the offspring being planned. This example underlines the fact that although considerable published information may be available to the manager on a subject, he must often, to be sure of its relevance to his particular situation, obtain the views of other experienced people in the field.

Financial

All four aspects of financial management as depicted in the diagram at the beginning of Chapter 9 are each dependent upon information. The preparation of the accounts and balance sheet summarising what *has* happened, require information, much of which should be readily available from the farm books. Budgeting and capital appraisal, both looking to the future, demand information from a wide range of sources both on and off the farm. As with technical information, relevance to the particular situation is of major importance. Financial data has a more private nature than most other kinds, and there is no substitute, in our minds, for good 'on the farm' data as a basis for future thinking.

The subject of borrowing will serve here as an example. Although the banks may regularly be advertising their services, it is not until the farmer makes a personal approach to his bank that he will, in fact, know if he is able to borrow, how much he will be allowed to borrow and on what terms. The response to a request will, no doubt, vary with time according to such factors as the national economic climate and the farmer's net worth. It will depend upon the feasibility of the particular project, the detailed way in which the proposal has been prepared and how relevant the figures are to the actual situation being discussed. The response may also vary from one bank to another; not that we suggest that farmers should regularly change their bankers. But we do wish to underline the fact that, if a farmer needs financial assistance from any lender, he will find that he probably has to do considerable homework before he can expect to obtain a positive response.

Legal

Managers of farms, as well as managers of other sectors of the economy, have to operate within the legal framework of the country in which they do business. The task of getting oneself acquainted with all the necessary legislation is not an easy one and it is made more difficult by constant additions and changes to the statute book. The law affects so many aspects of operating a farm of which taxation, employment, safety, road traffic and environmental planning are but a few. Ignorance is no longer an excuse, so that managers need to allocate some priority to this area of their work. Membership of such organisations as the Farmers Union or Producer Associations does prove valuable in obtaining expert advice and a file headed 'Useful Legal Information' is also worth keeping.

As an example, we take the legislation in the UK relating to trailer brakes. The law states that all trailers over a minimum weight need to be fitted with a braking system which can be operated from the tractor driver's seat. In practice, considerable difficulties arise with modern safety cabs as well as the need for quick release couplings when trailers are being constantly changed in, for instance, a silage making operation. Despite these problems, managers know that the safety of their drivers is of paramount importance, efficient trailer braking is imperative. To keep within the law in all situations may seem virtually impossible, but to be ignorant of it is, as we have said, no excuse.

International trade

A considerable range of inputs into the UK farm business are imported and an expanding number of commodities are sold into the world market. Some farmers will therefore need to have some awareness of the international market conditions, of exchange rates, levies and subsidies. Normally, they will not be dealing directly with an overseas customer but through a dealer as with machinery imports, or an agent as with exports. This middleman will, as part of his function, monitor the trading situation and provide this information to his clients as part of his service. Farmers may wish to back their own judgement and follow, for example, the international situation for a particular commodity (e.g. soya bean) before placing an order with their merchant. Similarly, lowland sheep farmers could observe the higher prices of, say, finished lamb that are being obtained in another country, especially for carcasses of a certain weight, confirmation and lean meat content. They might then consider ways of cashing in on such a trade and begin by evaluating new breeds of 'terminal' rams to produce the required carcasses. They may even need to look at such factors as a change of lambing date, feeding system or even breed of ewe in order to meet the needs of the buyer.

The Environment

As with the legal situation, the need to be aware of environmental requirements is an area of increasing significance to the farmer. Some aspects of this subject are covered by the law, whereas others involve doing the correct thing as a moral obligation to the community. In the UK, Codes of Practice are published in respect of such aspects as animal welfare and aerial spraying of pesticides. Another example of an activity covered by this heading is the burning of straw by arable farmers. A Code of Practice is available and considerable advisory information has been published on the subject. To follow the code precisely, no doubt causes considerable effort and inconvenience to the farmer and his staff. If short cuts are taken, then disasters are more likely to occur so that one day the practice may even be banned. There is always the concern, that in situations where the profit objective is given excess dominance that such corners are more likely to be cut. We, therefore, state again that there are objectives to running a farm business other than profits and an important one is that of caring for the environment.

SOURCES OF INFORMATION

A word or two now about the sources from which farmers obtain the information that they need. There is a wide variety. It is, therefore, important that each farmer explores by his own experience, and finds the most convenient sources for him, personally. Much will depend on how much time he is prepared to allocate to reading, making visits and attending conferences. Managers of small scale businesses may well be involved in manual chores for a large proportion of the working day and at other times are too tired to concentrate on serious reading.

Radio broadcasts on the other hand can be listened to while working, even in farm buildings or using portable sets in tractor cabs. Taped information is already available and could be more widely used especially by 'working' managers. Television is a good medium for gaining ideas but is seldom suited to obtaining detailed data. The use of videotapes could increase in the future, especially for training purposes.

The written word continues to be a major source of information and the farming industry especially in the UK, is well served with publications of many kinds. Many daily papers, especially provincial issues, carry farming information with reports, news and feature articles, but the popular weekly publications fulfil this role in a most comprehensive way. Specialised publications, usually on a monthly basis, deal well with many aspects of the major enterprises as well as machinery and management topics. A considerable proportion of this material is paid for by advertising revenue and is available free to farmers. This is perhaps a mixed blessing as free material more easily finds its way into the waste paper basket.

Numerous institutions including government, universities, and research institutes produce a comprehensive range of publications as do the Trade and the Banks. One problem is knowing what is available. The situation can be helped, however, by membership of an organisation, such as, in the UK, The British Institute of Management which produces lists of available information and literature reviews.

MARKET INTELLIGENCE DATA

This subject has been touched on in a previous chapter but, we feel, is important enough to deserve special mention here. It embraces several different kinds of information. The agricultural industry in many countries, but especially in the UK, is well served with a market reporting service. Material is available from the farming and local press, in radio broadcasts, as well as from telephone dial-in recorded messages. Usually, this information reports recent sale prices with some indication as to type or grade of commodity. Many producers are in direct contact with the market on a regular basis in respect of both buying and selling so do not need to study such published material.

In general, there is a lack of information available to farmers about expected market situations in the future. Such information is required when planning production and when making investment decisions. If such information were available, no doubt this would cause over-reaction with many commodities and the outcome would be very different to that first predicted. Hunt, in the article in *Farm Management* referred to at the end of this chapter, suggests two promising lines of approach to overcome this problem. First, to set up reporting arrangements to keep track of response and to report continuously. The MAFF quarterly report goes some way towards this in respect of critical items such as in-pig gilts. Secondly, he suggests that products which are subject to 'over response' could be increasingly marketed through groups or co-operatives which have a ready contact with the changing state of the market.

The task of obtaining all the necessary marketing information and interpreting it correctly is not an easy one. It is also time consuming so that many farmers may be well advised to concentrate on production and to delegate the major part of marketing to the specialists. These may be enthusiastic leaders of producer groups – for buying and/or selling, full time employees of co-operatives or specialised marketing consultants. Seldom will the official adviser consider that this type of activity comes 'into his court'.

STORAGE AND RETRIEVAL

It may well be common practice in the future, for a farmer to obtain information for a particular purpose by the use of a telephone link to a central, or even a local, computer. The data will be obtained as a print-out, or by display on a modified TV receiver. (e.g. Viewdata). Broadcasting authorities are already offering a wide range of televised data sheets. It may be that he requires data relating to his own business or to the national or even to the international situation. In the meantime, and perhaps for some time it will be necessary to accumulate all such required information in the farm office. A good, usable, system of filing data is essential. It may be based on individual cost items or enterprises. Frankly, we would not wish to be categoric about this. It is very much a matter for the individual. But what he must be able to do is to 'access' whatever data and information he collects as and when he needs it. Such data needs to be kept up-to-date and to be readily available for reference. Some managers consider the analysis of farm data to be a job that they need to do personally as it helps them to quickly pinpoint areas needing control action. Others delegate this task to office staff and make decisions based on summaries. There is a real need for the person collating and analysing farm data to have the necessary skills and experience as accuracy is vital. This may well involve close contact with staff who collect the raw data, so as to be in a position to quickly clear any queries that may arise.

Information received from outside the business has also to be stored, but yet be available for speedy reference. Filing of journals and market reports by date of issue causes few problems, but more difficult is the retrieval of an interesting article on a particular topic read in a magazine months ago. We find considerable value in keeping a set of box files labelled by enterprise or subject. Such interesting articles which may be of use in the future are cut or torn out at the time of reading and stored in this way. Piles of back numbers of journals and magazines that you intend to read, have a habit of growing uncontrollably high.

ADVISERS

We have discussed in earlier chapters the valuable role that an outsider can have in assisting a manager to set clear objectives and in planning the strategy for his business. Now we can consider the wider role of the adviser or consultant. Amongst the most important contributions that he can offer are:

(a) Specialist technical information, such as the identification of crop disease and recommendations for control. Such a specialist may well be retained by a group of producers to visit their farmers on a regular basis and offer assistance very much at production level in respect of selection of inputs and timeliness of operations.
(b) Guidance on technical aspects, especially in relation to setting up a new enterprise, including full feasibility studies. The inseparability of technical and managerial aspects of farming may require the expertise of a widely experienced consultant.
(c) Advice of a strictly economic nature, perhaps involving analysis of past performance, or future planning or questions of capital procurement and appraisal.
(d) The use of his 'trained eye' to give opinion, either to confirm the views of the farmer or to help overcome the fact that the farmer may be too close to his business to view it objectively.
(e) Specialised guidance in one of the more complicated aspects

of business management, such as taxation or recruitment of staff.
(f) Regular consultations over a period of time to assist in the implementation of control procedures.

Regular contact with an adviser can build a relationship of mutual trust and understanding so that follow-up advice becomes even more valuable. As time progresses, the advice will often become more involved with the whole farm business so that the outside influence is then considerable.

CONCLUSION

The amount of information that any farmer might need and the range of sources from which he can try to find it presents a rather frightening prospect. What we have tried to suggest in this chapter is that each individual needs to think his way through this topic and devise a strategy to meet his own needs and circumstances. In any particular situation there are certain obvious needs and certain obvious sources. The individual would do well to identify and concentrate on these; to set his own priorities. Sometimes the required information will come from deliberate attempts to collect it, at other times it will be a by-product of some other activity: a discussion, farm walk or the like. It is important for each individual to learn how much time he can afford - and how much he cannot afford - to spend on this kind of activity. To under-involve himself - or to over-involve himself - to the detriment of his many other chores, could be dangerous, and we do not pretend that finding the right balance, or the right source, is at all easy.

SOME QUESTIONS RELATING TO THIS CHAPTER

(1) What kind of agricultural information do you find most difficult to obtain?
(2) How could you improve your office filing system?
(3) 'British farmers suffer from an oversupply of information'. Do you agree?
(4) Which of your farm products would you consider to be 'volatile' in respect of supply and demand?
(5) If you were to sell one of your major products on a contract arrangement, do you have adequate information to prepare a negotiating brief?

(6) What type of adviser could be of most use to you in increasing farm profits?

A GUIDE TO SELECTED FURTHER READING

Hunt, K. E. 1974. Market Intelligence – Which Way Now? *Farm Management* **2,** no. 8, 435–41.
    A valuable article for readers interested in the use of information relating to the marketing function.
Management Information, 1978. London: BIM.
    A comprehensive catalogue of BIM publications.
Giles, A. K. 1970. Management Consultants. *Agriculture* **77,** no. 11, 525–8.
    This short article discusses the need for and value of farm advice.
Brown, D. 1973. Farm Office Organisation. *Farm Management* **2,** no. 5.
    A useful guide to office procedures.

13
Priorities

> First of all, I will...?

THE IMPORTANCE OF PRIORITIES

This chapter is a special one and apart from the Summary and Conclusion, it is the last one. It is also the shortest and, in many ways, may be the most important. It is about getting the most important things done.

In his stimulating book, The Effective Executive, Peter Drucker suggests that it is possible for executives to actually develop habits of mind which will help to make them more effective; that over and above the normal attributes of intelligence, imagination and knowledge, effectiveness can be learned. He lists five habits of mind to be cultivated in order to help bring this situation about. One of these five is to identify priorities and to stay with them. In order to try to capture something of the full flavour of what Drucker has to say on this topic we have strung together some of his phrases from the relevant chapter:

> 'effective executives concentrate on the few major areas where superior performance will produce outstanding results ... They know that they have no choice but to do first things first and second things not at all. The alternative is to get nothing done ... If there is any one 'secret' of effectiveness, it is concentration. Effective executives do first things first and they do one thing at a time ... most of us find it hard enough to do well even one thing at a time, let alone two ... those people who do so many things and apparently so many difficult things

... do only one at a time. As a result they need much less time in the end than the rest of us ... Effective executives do not race. They set an easy pace but keep going steadily.'

We find ourselves in total sympathy with these views and know the importance in our own work of being selective; of identifying priorities. This theme has already run through a number of chapters in this book. It was implicit, for instance, in all that was written about setting objectives – the need to identify what one is aiming at both personally and professionally. The jigsaw of objectives at the head of that chapter is essentially about priorities. They appear again in the context of decision making when, sooner or later, a choice between alternatives has to be made; also in the chapter on Planning in order to avoid management by crisis; and yet again in the chapter on Control in the identification of key results areas; keeping tabs on what really matters.

Nevertheless it is felt that the subject is so important – so close to the heart of good management – that it must be singled out for special and separate treatment in this penultimate chapter. The process is, of course, easier said than done.

THE NATURE OF PRIORITIES

It will no doubt help the reader if we state what kind of priorities we have in mind here, for there are several.

First, there are those *broad priorities related to long term strategies*. 'What is needed', says Drucker elsewhere in his book, 'is the right strategy rather than razzle dazzle tactics'. This interpretation of a priority is virtually synonymous with the concept of management by objectives. Organising a business or ordering your own personal life means identifying priorities. 'Get your priorities right', we say to each other when discussing broad questions of what matters to us and what does not. It is important, as we noted in our chapters on Objectives and on Managing the Manager, to make enough time available to consider the important things. No manager who wishes to be effective must become too busy dealing with the *urgent* to deal with the *important*. Getting the farm plan right, over the next four or five years is, for instance, important.

Within these broad strategies, there is a second kind of priority: *identifying the critical areas of a business* – what really makes it tick – and keeping careful control over them. As we have already stated earlier in the book, it is very often the case that only a very few key result areas (one, two or three) are the critical ones in determining whether ultimate profits are good, bad or indifferent in a particular year. These priority areas should be identified and given all the managerial time and effort that they demand: food conversion in a factory enterprise; cultivations and the management of plant growth on a cereals farm; milk yield and stocking density in the dairy. Budgetary control, discussed in Chapter 6, is very much about this aspect of management; about doing the important things well.

A third kind of priority relates closely to decision making of the kind illustrated in Chapter 5. At particular points of time, in the middle of a production cycle, problems arise and a *choice between alternatives has to be made*. Do you press on with a suspect machine or stop to get it repaired? By what method will you harvest those potatoes in unusually wet conditions? Do you stop an important job to do another (e.g. repair a broken fence) which may, or may not, create further problems? These are the more pressing and immediate situations in which, 'what matters most', has to be identified and dealt with.

There is, finally, a fourth kind of priority situation, when, for instance, a real *crisis* occurs, perhaps involving personal accident or fire. In these cases priorities become starkly clear. There is no real problem of choice; everything else stops.

ORDERING THE PRIORITIES

It is impossible to offer detailed guidance on this question; answers will vary according to individuals and circumstances. Sometimes, as in our fourth kind of situation, answers really will be starkly clear; sometimes, as in the first, they will emerge only after prolonged thought and discussions. In between, situations requiring constant control and firm decisions will require concentration and application. It may help, however, to keep in mind two points. First, the simple question, 'What really matters?'. Robert Townsend tells us in Up the Organisation that he keeps a sign opposite his desk which reads, 'Is what I'm doing or about to do getting us closer to our objectives?'. Try applying that question when you next have to decide on a priority. What may also help is to remember that what is deferred very often diminishes in importance and sometimes does not get done at all. If you do not believe us, what about all those articles and reports that you have put on one side to read later? The problem confronting most managers is not simply a matter of selecting the most important task; there are usually too many of those to chose from. It is more often a question of deciding which ones will matter least if they do not get done.

STICKING WITH PRIORITIES

Remembering Drucker's advice about doing one thing at a time, we wish, finally, in this chapter to stress the importance of concentrating on priorities once they have been identified. If this is not done the whole process will have been a waste of time. On most farms, with their several enterprises, with the problems of distance and the risk of interruptions discussed in Chapter 11, there is plenty of scope for getting diverted. A lot of time can be spent – and wasted – turning and moving from one job to another. Concentrating on one until it is finished – especially when it has priority – and then moving to the next job on the list has much to commend it. There are those who work well when they have several jobs in hand at the same time, but the possibility of none of them being satisfactorily completed must always be there. In our own experience we are aware of the beneficial effect on morale of actually finishing a job, especially if it has been done well. There is a better chance of that being the case if other things have not been allowed to interfere. We have always found that lists of jobs are a valuable aid to getting things in the right order of priority and then getting them done. Crossing jobs off the list is very satisfying, and prevents it from just getting longer and longer. The reader should not be apologetic about a list, nor let other people decide for him what should go on it; he should keep his priorities under review – they can change from day to day – and not let others prevent him from completing jobs. If the list just gets longer and longer it's time to do some more delegating.

SOME QUESTIONS RELATING TO THIS CHAPTER

(1) What are the most important priorities in the long term strategic plans for your business?
(2) To what extent are your personal priorities and those of your family compatible with your business plan?
(3) How do you go about deciding on your day-to-day priorities?
(4) Do you stick at a job until it is completed? Or are you too easily diverted?
(5) Do you keep systematic lists of what you have to do?
(6) Do crises often occur in your business?
(7) Do you always seem to be in a hurry?

A GUIDE TO SELECTED FURTHER READING

Drucker, P. F. 1970. *The Effective Executive*. London: Heinemann; London: Pan Books.
  Read Chapter 5 (First things first), but the whole book is priceless. Get it – and read it – regularly.

14
Summary and conclusions

In this final chapter it is proposed to do two things. First, to summarise briefly what has been written in each chapter and to leave with the reader a final thought on each subject. Quite apart from bringing together the main threads and philosophy of the book, it is felt that this device might assist the reader who, having read the whole book once, might at some subsequent date, wish to refresh his memory of its contents. The diagrams at the front of each chapter and the questions at the end may serve a similar purpose. Secondly, by way of conclusion, there are a few final general thoughts that we wish to express.

SUMMARY

PART I INTRODUCTION

Chapter 1 About this book

This chapter begins with a consideration of profits. Profits provide a measure of success, a means of reward, and a fund for expansion.

They encourage and permit survival. Profits vary enormously between farms of different sizes and types, but also between farms that are similar to each other. This variation is due to a combination of physical and human factors and it is suggested that it is the capacity of the manager for personal and professional growth which may be the most flexible element in the whole complex that makes up a farm business.

This book has been written essentially for those managers and is about the job that they do. It has not been about husbandry or economics or operational research, but about the management of farm businesses. It has endeavoured to concentrate on those aspects of management which seem to us to worry farm managers and which they find most difficult to order in their minds. The reader will have therefore found ways of thinking rather than answers; directions but not decisions.

Our final thought: farm management is a task performed only by managers of farms. It is not undertaken by those who write about it, teach it or give advice on it.

Chapter 2 About management

Management is defined as a comprehensive activity, involving the combination of human, physical and financial resources in a way which produces a commodity or a service which is both wanted and can be offered at a price which will be paid, while making the working environment for those involved agreeable and acceptable. This definition emphasises that management is a comprehensive activity without narrow boundaries; that it is concerned with the combination of different kinds of resources; that it must be market orientated; and that there must be an emphasis on the human factor. It involves setting objectives, making plans, taking decisions and exercising control. The main sectors of most businesses that have to be managed are those of production, marketing, finance and staffing. None of this takes place divorced from a wider environment.

Our final thought: that it is maybe more helpful to think in terms of management applied to farms than of farm management as a subject in its own right; farmers and farm managers should avoid thinking of themselves as managerially unique.

PART II MANAGEMENT FUNCTIONS

Chapter 3 Setting objectives

It is claimed that setting objectives is a very important task, but also a difficult one. Some more or less formal application of the principles of management by objectives will almost certainly help. This will involve a thorough examination of the internal and external environments and some self examination. It will take time and will need repeating. Objectives will change over time and there will always be conflicting priorities, not least, the need to do things well *now* and the need to think well for the *future*.

Our final thought: Success will not follow just because objectives have been set. It will follow if those objectives are good ones and if, as far as possible, they are then achieved.

Chapter 4 Planning

Planning is closely related to the setting of objectives, but is separate from it. Plans formalise the way in which objectives can be pursued. Planning involves giving time to something *before* it happens so that influence can be exercised over it *when* it happens. Managers should try to control events and not be controlled by events; they should avoid management by crisis. Planning is relevant to all sectors and problems in a business, not just the production programme: examples have been given. Planning may or may not involve the use of planning techniques. Plans may be strategic or day-to-day. They often do not work out as planned. One is seldom planning from scratch; more often making adjustments to existing plans.

Our final thought: Having the peace of mind that stems from a plan usually allows more flexibility with which to cope with unforeseen events, rather than less; everyday human attributes such as thoroughness, orderliness and judgement will play a major part in the process.

Chapter 5 Decision making

Decisions convert plans and thoughts into action. Without decisions there would be no productive process at all. The manager's function is sometimes thought of as being characterised by the decision making function. Decisions (including when to do nothing), have to be made continually; they can have far reaching results and, on a day-to-day basis, influence how well things are actually done. What is required is *good* decisions; it can never be known if decisions have been the *best* possible. Decisions can be strategic or tactical: examples of each are given. Decision making is not synonymous with problem-solving, it is principally about *selection* between alternatives. Formally, the process involves: identifying the issue; assessing its significance; considering alternatives; collecting information; evaluating the information; making a choice; implementation; checking results; and, finally, accepting responsibility.

Our final thought: A good manager learns to recognise when an issue or problem deserves his time and he then gives it; judgement will be an important ingredient in the process.

Chapter 6   Control

Control is an important subject because it concerns actually getting things done – and done properly. The need for control is continuous. It is especially important in a multi-enterprise business when a good performance in one part can easily mask a poor performance in another. Control in a day-to-day sense is essentially a physical matter involving the careful employment of people and materials. At appropriate points during and at the end of the year it has a financial budgetary element, involving the checking of performance against targets. Targets must be realistic. Budgetary control provides the most pertinent yardstick available to management. Some farm enterprises (the 'factory' type) lend themselves to frequent short period checks, while others (arable, livestock rearing) do not. Similarly, some inputs (the 'stream' type) do and some (the 'tap' type) do not. Budgetary control uses arithmetic but is not primarily about arithmetic, it is about management.

Our final thought: Effective control requires measurement, and, when necessary and possible, corrective action; without this action there is no control. There is probably more scope for increasing profits on most farms by a more careful control of the existing system than from radically changing it.

PART III WHAT HAS TO BE MANAGED

Chapter 7 Production

Production actually brings commodities into being. It is a complex notion and process, involving the co-ordination of all forms of capital and labour. At any point of time, producers of agricultural commodities will be concerned with achieving economic efficiency, not just technical efficiency irrespective of 'effective demand'. They will have to decide what to produce, by what methods and in what combination.

Three separate aspects of production are considered: building up a farm plan (using various techniques ranging in their degree of sophistication); acquiring and allocating the resources that are not already available on the farm, or for which there is competing demand; and operating the farm plan through the maintenance of technical standards and the supervision of staff.

Of the various techniques that can be used in preparing a farm plan, a preference is expressed for some form of 'ordered budgeting' using gross margins. A systematic approach to adjusting the production plan is also discussed, along with a brief appraisal of the gross margin measurement.

Our final thought: a vital aspect of any production programme lies in determining the genuine limits to each enterprise. Changes in economic circumstances have often been known to create changes in farming thinking.

Chapter 8 Buying and selling

From the consumer's point of view nothing has been finally produced until it reaches the point where it can be purchased, i.e. until it has utility. Production and marketing are therefore simply two parts of a continuous chain and the farmer is one member of that chain. Many of them feel the urge to become more actively involved in the marketing end of the chain, but suspect that they cannot compete in marketing as a professional, specialised, commercial operation. But they are making marketing decisions when they make production decisions; they must decide what, where, when and how to sell. Examples of a crop and a livestock situation are given. Buying also involves knowledge of markets and usually occurs more frequently than selling. In the broad sense, farmers are involved in marketing whether they like it or not; they need to be informed and they need to decide, in their own circumstances, what kind of a link in the chain they want to be.

Our final thought: Keeping up to date on the outlook and market trends may be a valuable exercise if it only serves to encourage an individual in believing that he is doing the right things and to go on doing them as well as he can; although this should not blind him to the possible need for change.

Chapter 9 Finance

To the businessman, capital means resources, whether they take the form of land, labour, or capital in the economist's sense. Using capital is, therefore, what farming is about.

Examining *past trade* involves good records and a sufficiently detailed trading account so that meaningful measures of performance can be made. Intra-farm comparisons – using gross margins – may be more helpful than inter-farm comparisons, and there may be some limited use for net margin calculations. *Future trading* prospects can be assessed by budgets cast in various forms depending on the questions to be answered. The partial budget is the most frequently needed of these tools. Cash flows have a special role in assessing the effect of transactions on bank balances.

The *past capital* position will be recorded in the balance sheet, showing the deployment of capital and its ownership. To have an overall understanding of the balance sheet is more valuable than to be equipped with a wide range of balance sheet ratios. The *future use of capital* involves some form of investment appraisal, a part of which should be quantitative and part of which, in the nature of things, will not be. A ten-point investment check list is suggested.

Our final thought: It may help a prospective borrower to prepare his case if he thinks himself into the position of the prospective lender.

Chapter 10 Staff

The quantitative and qualitative importance of labour are discussed in this chapter. Present needs may not always be matched by the present work force. Staff planning is designed to bring the two into line and anticipate future needs. Getting the right man into the right job is all important. It will be aided by a systematic approach to job evaluation, recruitment and induction. Subsequently, attention to all aspects of motivation, training and leadership will be the cornerstones of successful employment. If, for any reason, it is necessary to reduce staff, this should be approached as painstakingly as when a new member of staff is taken on.

Our final thought: There is no more important job that a manager or farmer does than when he takes on a new member of staff. No stone should be left unturned to try to ensure that it is done successfully.

PART IV   THE MANAGER

Chapter 11   Managing the manager

The importance of the 'head' of any organisation is stressed. The farmer is part and parcel of the farm's resources that have to be managed. Although managers may have many individual differences of background, training and financial circumstances, they have many managerial problems in common. These problems tend to stem from their relative isolation, the fragmentation of their time, and the feeling, too often we suggest, of their being indispensable. At the same time a manager can, because of the relatively small scale nature of his business, be under-employed – even bored – in a strict managerial sense. It is important that individuals face up to these possible difficulties and find solutions. Solutions will depend upon individual circumstances and inclinations. Personal and professional growth are at stake and so is the efficiency with which all other resources on the farm are managed.

Our final thought: There is no short cut to competence. Education, training, experience on the job and contact with others all play their part, and with them comes *judgement*.

Conclusions

Chapter 12   Acquiring information

Reference is made to the different kinds of information that are needed by farm managers (technical, financial, legal, etc.) and to the different sources from where it will be sought (government, research establishments, universities and colleges, the media, etc.). Special reference is made to market intelligence data, to its uses and limitations. The important question of information retrieval systems in farm offices is discussed with the emphasis on simplicity and usage. Finally the importance of people as sources of information and help is considered, and the need to learn discrimination in seeking such help.

Our final thought: What farm managers need is not *data*. They need *information* that will be useful to them. They need to learn where to get it, how to store it and how to use it.

Chapter 13   Priorities

'Setting priorities and staying with them', is one of the five habits of mind with which Drucker believes managers can help to train themselves to become more effective. The topic has featured in several previous chapters of this book. Here, because of its special importance it is given a short chapter to itself. After establishing the importance of the subject, different kinds of priorities are considered ranging from long term strategic ones to those of the immediate crisis type. Then some practical issues are dealt with, such as the way to select priorities, the need for staying with jobs until they are completed and the need to review priorities from time to time.

Our final thought: That Drucker was right!

CONCLUSIONS

We come finally to a number of after-thoughts and reactions which we would like to express before laying down our pens. They are not specially related to each other, so we shall just list them.

(a)   We have been conscious throughout the writing of this book of its omissions and the fact that we deliberately turned our backs on the inclusion of techniques and figures. The book may be unique for that, if for no other reasons. There may be readers who regret that they have not found more illustrations of our theme, more husbandry recommendations and more economic theory. If so, we can only plead that such a book would not have been the book that we wanted to write. Our sights were set firmly on the managerial problems that confront farmers and managers. We wanted to provide guidelines not answers, directions not decisions. Whatever other shortcomings our efforts may have, we feel that we can at least claim to have kept our word.

(b) We have also been conscious of the inter-locking nature of our subject and the possibility, therefore, of some duplication of thought. We have been unable to avoid this, and indeed, had we done so, may have wrongly portrayed a subject whose component parts are inter-dependent and inter-locking. And every part of it does seem to us to be equally important. Yet we have been aware that as we have approached each chapter it has seemed to be the most important of them all. Several times we have claimed for different topics – control, production, and finance, for instance, that they are 'at the heart of farming'. The truth of the matter is that each of them is.

(c) It has long been the case that both of us have possessed a very healthy respect for those who manage commercial farms. Their job is complex; it requires a wide range of expertise and they are, relatively speaking, alone in the managerial role. As we have written this book, and literally spelt out the full complexity of that job, our respect for those involved is increased. But we do not weep for them; those of them whom we know seem to enjoy their lives, despite the problems. We simply respect them for the job that they do.

(d) We also respect their wives. Those of them who might glance through this book (we recommend Chapter 11) may feel that they have had very little mention. That is true and we apologise to them. They were not one of the deliberate omissions. It is rather that they would require another book to themselves. We are certainly not unmindful of the supremely important roles they play ranging from simply 'holding the fort' to helping 'to get priorities right'. As onlookers they see so much of the game.

(e) There is one respect in which we hope that we will not be misinterpreted by the reader. It is this: our book has been about management *for managers, not for, or in order to try to create, super-managers*. We do not envisage that anyone who reads it will want to rush away to embark on an orgy of objective setting, planning, decision making and control. What we hope is that some encouragement and some guidelines have been provided that will be of some assistance when those jobs have to be done, as surely they must be. And although the book was written essentially for practising farmers and managers it may be that it will offer some help to other managers who might read it.

(f) There has been limited mention of computers in what we have written and that might surprise some. The reason for that is simple. What we have offered is for the farmer-manager himself. We know that there are some who make direct use of computers but we believe them to be exceptional. Vast use is made of computers in the agricultural industry at large, ranging from global purposes to the exploration of on-farm methods of planning and control. A wide range of such techniques now exists including the long standing tool for prescribing the mix of ingredients for commercially compounded animal feeds. It would be our contention, however, that the computer has yet to invade the farm as such on any scale. The situation may be different in a few years from now, but we cannot be sure.

(g) If one word, perhaps more than any other, has been used again and again in this book it is the word 'judgement'. It is not easy to define; it is close to the word 'discretion'. It suggests an ability to weigh up any situation – the quantifiable and the non quantifiable elements – and to reach a decision that at the very least proves not to be bad. It may well be that the ability of a manager to do just that is his most important quality; more important even than to achieve a particular profit level. It is very important, therefore, that self-employed managers should assume, and that salaried managers should be given, the authority that permits them fully to exercise their discretion and judgement. Managers, in short, *must* manage; they must be allowed to, and must train themselves to.

(h) We should not end, however, with even the slightest suggestion that profits are anything but very important. On occasions they may take second place, but over time, it is profits, as we stated in Chapter 1, which permit survival. None of the subject matter of this book is important for itself. Each subject is part of a means to an end. It is all part and parcel of effective management which will become reflected – within the talents and capabilities of all the individuals involved – in an ability to generate profits, to permit growth and to enable a business and its employment opportunities to continue. Profitability was the note on which this book opened and on which we have also chosen to end it.

Index

In order to facilitate easy and helpful use, this index has been restricted deliberately to the *main* concepts and topics that have been discussed and page references have, in the main, been limited to those parts of the text where the items listed have been given their principal consideration or mention. No names of other authors have been included in this index, but any author whose work has been referred to in the text has also been included in the appropriate 'guide to selected further reading'. With one or two exceptions, the material contained in the final chapter, most of which summarises what has preceded it, has also been excluded from the index.

acquiring resources   86–91, 101–2
advisers–consultants   83, 116, 122, 127, 131, 134, 139, 177, 178–9
analysis of trading results   122–3
assets   132–5, 136

balance sheets   132–5
   limitations of   135
   ratios   134–5
budgetary control   61–9
budgeting   62–3
   break-even   129
   cash flows   129–32
   complete   126–7
   difficulties of   126, 131–2
   need for different kinds   129
   partial   33, 48, 85, 108–9, 128
buying   101–2

capital
   definitions   114
   in balance sheet   133, 135
   return on   135–42
   types of   136
cash flows   65, 129–32
communications   152–3
comparative analysis   68, 121–3
complete budgets   126–7
computers   66, 79, 131, 195
contractors   90
control   59–70
   essence of   61–2
   importance of   60–1
   need for action   67–8
   physical nature of   64
   use of budgets in:
      annual   64
      short period   64–6
costs, *see* inputs *and* fixed costs

decision making   43–58, 107–9
   adequate time for   50
   components of   46–9

examples of:
   strategic decision   50–5
   tactical decision   55–8
delegation   165–6
diminishing returns   78, 82

economic efficiency   75–6
effective demand   75, 103
effectiveness   20, 181–2
efficiency measures   121–3
enterprise budgets–accounts   85, 123–6
equilibrium   76–7
excluded material   5–6, 193–4
external environment   25

Farm Management Pocketbook   85
financial management   113–42
   accounts   117–26
   balance sheets   132–7
   budgets and cash flows   126–32
   diagrammatic view of   115–16
   financial planning, example   37–8
   investment appraisal   137–42
fixed costs   81, 82–3, 84–5, 124–6

gearing   133
gross margin(s)   78–80, 82–5, 124–5, 128
   normalised gross margins   80
group trading   102–3, 177

incentive payments   141
information for managers   171–80
   kinds of:
      environmental   175
      financial   173
      intelligence   176–7
      international   174
      legal   173–4
      technical   172
   need for   171
   sources of   175–6
   storage and retrieval   177–8

Index

inputs 119–20, 121–3
input: output ratios 120
intended readership 4–5, 195
interest 141
investment appraisal 137–42
  authors' checklist 140
  discounted yield 139
  intuitive approach 139
  net present value 139
  pay-back period 138
  return on outlay 138

job description 146–7
job satisfaction 144
judgement 33, 49, 50, 78, 109, 132, 195

key results areas 22, 24, 69, 183

labour management 143–56
labour profiles 145–6
leadership 152–3
liabilities 132–5
linear programming 79
lists of jobs 184

management
  by crisis 31
  by objectives 21–3
  diagramatic view of 13–15
  definition of 10–12
management accounting 118–20
management and investment income 136
managers
  individuality of 162–3
  influence of 160
  personal problems of 163–8
    boredom 163–4
    delegating 165–6
    insecurity 167
    isolation 163
    organisation of time 164–5
    long, irregular hours 166
    recreational needs 166–7
    under-employment 164
  self appraisal of 25, 160–1
  their role 13–15, 95
managers' wives 194–5
marketing 97–111, 176–7
  farmers role in 99–101, 103, 109–11
  planning of, example 33–9
  relationship to production 98–9, 102–3
market intelligence data 107–9, 176–7

marginal cost 77
marginal revenue 77
motivation 151–2

net margin 125
net worth 133–5

objectives 19–29
  advantages of 24–5
  determination of 21–3
  difficulties of 26–8
  long and short term 26
  management by 21–3
  need for 20–1
  personal 27
operating production plans 91–5
opportunity costs 108
ordered budgeting 80
output 119–20, 121–3
overtrading 133

partial budgeting 33, 48, 85, 108–9, 128
performance:
  gap 3–4, 68–9
  judgements about 121
  targets 62–3
  technical 11, 93–5
personal development 160–1
planning 30–42
  adjustments to 33
  examples of:
    employment 40–1
    finance 37–8
    marketing 38–9
    production 35–7
  failure of 33
  nature of 31–4
  time spent 34
priorities 93, 181–5
  importance of 181–2
  nature of 182–3
  ordering of 183–4
  sticking with 184–5
profit 3–4, 117–18, 136, 196
  methods of improving 81–3
  sharing 152
profit and loss accounts 117–18
programme planning 80
production 73–96
  complexity of 73–4
  devising production plans 78–81
    computerised methods 79
    programme planning methods 78–80

production—*continued*
  devising production plans—*contd.*
    subjective methods 78
    essential parts of 75
    operating the production plan 91–5
    production planning, example 35–7
    relationship to marketing 98–9, 102–3

records 119, 123
recruiting staff 146–8
redundancy 154
resources
  acquiring them 86–91, 101–2
  appraisal of 24–5
  flexibility of 4
retirement of staff 153–4
return on capital 135–42
  existing 135–7
  fresh injections 137–42

selling 102–3
  examples of:
    crops 105–7
    livestock 103–5
sensitivity analysis 129
specialists 90, 116
square-one questions 24

staff 143–156
  communications 152–3
  disengagement 153–5
  induction 148
  motivation and leadership 151–3
  payment 152
  planning 144–6
  recruiting and interviewing 146–8
  supervision 95
  training 149–51
standards of performance 121–2
standard man days 145

taxation 116–17
technical efficiency 75–6, 84
theory of the firm 76–8
trading accounts 117–18, 124
  adjustment to 121
training 149–51
  management 150
  skills 149
  supervisory 150

uncertainty and risk 33–4, 94, 129, 135
utility 98, 103

variable costs, *see* gross margin